In Search of the
New Age

In Search of the
New Age

by Christopher S. Kilham
Illustrated by Robert Engman

Destiny Books
Rochester, Vermont

Destiny Books
One Park Street
Rochester, Vermont 05767

Library of Congress Cataloging-in-Publication Data
Kilham, Christopher.
    In search of the new age.

    1. New Age movement—Anecdotes, facetiae, satire, etc.
I. Engman, Robert.   II. Title.
BP605.N48K55   1988   133'.0207   88–3810
ISBN 0—89281—209—5

              10 9 8 7 6 5 4 3 2 1

Destiny Books is a division of Inner Traditions International, Ltd.

Printed and bound in the United States.
Distributed to the book trade in the United States by
Harper and Row Publishers, Inc.
Distributed to the book trade in Canada by
Book Center, Inc., Montreal, Quebec

Contents

Acknowledgments

To Kate, of course.
Tighten your seat belt, honey—the road gets tricky from here.
Thanks:
To Craig Weatherby for editorial support. When are we going to Burma?
To Rob Engman, artist supreme.
To Joseph Jochmans, for permission to use a number of his titles
in The New Age Book List.
To A. C. Gallo, Jimmy Lewis, Joseph Jochmans, Ehud Sperling, Del Riddle,
Steven Josephs, Jack Casey, and Ed Conroy for contributions.
To Gene Kilham, for engendering strange brainwaves.
To Mom, for bearing me and bearing with me.
To Richard Bandler, for the technology of fun.
To Anthony Harnett, for unflagging support.
To the folks at Kailuum, a little piece of paradise on the Yucatán coast,
where a lot of these ideas were born, between cool beers, Mayan food, and
fantastic company.
And to Laura Inouye, Steve and Aureet Hassan, Estella Arias, and Leslie
Colket, for everything you've all done for me, which is plenty.

Introduction

FOR THE LAST decade or more, the term *New Age* has been bandied about liberally, in conversations, publications, and in broadcast media. But what is the New Age? Is it a period in time? Is it a collection of ideas? Or is it an emerging culture whose shared values and ideas are spawning a vast array of philosophies, products, services, and activities?

Whatever the New Age is, one thing is certain. This phenomenon has insinuated itself deeply into our culture. It has become part of the warp and woof of our social fabric. We speak of good vibes, organic foods, karma, acupuncture, and spiritual masters, as though these had always been part of our language and lifestyle. Yet such is not the case. The emergence of the "New Age" represents one of the most rapidly growing trends ever observed in modern history.

In Search of the New Age is a project that developed out of a need to understand this trend and to detail some of its key components. Over a period of twenty-four months, a team of us investigated the ideas, products, and personalities of the New Age. This catalog is the distillation of what for all of us has been an intriguing and enlightening journey. For easy reference, the catalog is divided into eight chapters, from Services to Products. Each chapter contains information and commentary provided by our editorial staff.

To defray the costs of publication, we have accepted advertising from socially responsible groups and companies. We have been as selective as possible, with regard to the inclusion of both advertisements and category listings. At the same time, we have attempted not to be unduly biased or exclusionary. We cannot guarantee the authenticity of all information in the catalog and therefore advise you to exercise good judgment in the selection of any products or services found here. We also encourage your feedback. After all, we are all the New Age!

The Editorial Staff of *In Search of the New Age:*

Ben Dover: An expert in holistic health and tribal cultures, Ben has traveled extensively throughout Asia and South America, studying ethnopharmacology, the medicine of various cultures. A native of Seattle, Ben is also a fully trained shaman, having studied for eight years with the legendary Huichol medicine man don Bernardo Tuchus.

Wanda Round: A consummate artisan and craftsperson, Wanda hails from Boulder, Colorado, where she ran an artists' co-op before joining our staff. Wanda describes herself as "a free spirit trying to come to terms with gravity." She is the author of two books on macramé, including the best-selling *Low-Tech Suspension Bridges* and *Knot on Your Life.* Wanda is also a devotee of Bindu Yin Yang and is an expert on spiritual traditions. She stopped casting a shadow in 1968.

Bing Lifschitz: This Connecticut Yankee is a hard-bitten journalist, and former public radio reporter. His most popular expressions are "Let's get right down to the facts" and "Can I have the other half of your sandwich?" Bing has written for the *Hartford Courant, Yankee Magazine, Structural Houseplants Monthly, Gerbil Breeder's Digest,* and *The Valley Advocate.* Bing is an avid hunter, jogger, and Zen golf enthusiast. His article "Nuts, Berries, and Flakes in the Health Food Movement" won a Hugo Ralph award.

Indianola Bunch: A graduate of Pasadena Junior College, where she majored in philosophy, Indianaola is also an oenologist (wine expert) and brewmaster. This Sacramento native has personally visited virtually every significant holistic center in the United States, about which she comments, "It's enough to make you cuckoo." Indianola became our first staff member after agents from the Bureau of Alcohol, Tobacco, and Firearms closed her unlicensed brewery.

C. C. Rider: This professor of comparative religions bagged his job at Indlana State University and took a two-year motorcycle trip through Europe before joining us. A martial artist and Yoga enthusiast, C. C. is also a collector of rare tapes and records, and owns the only known complete collection of the concerts of Sri Chinmoy. He is a gourmet chef and a third cousin to Detroit's Mitch Rider.

About the Illustrations:

We're basically an ecology-minded bunch here. We fully intended to include photographs of the various people and products described in this catalog. But when we considered the toxic chemicals used in photo developing, we realized that we had no choice but to illustrate the catalog with original art. To accomplish this, we turned to the very talented Max McGraw.

Max "Quick-Draw" McGraw: This native of Tunisia did a six-year stint in the French Foreign Legion prior to finishing his graduate work at Rhode Island School of Design. McGraw's illustrations have appeared in *Time*, *Atlantic Monthly*, and *Playboy* magazines. An expert in Filipino stick fighting, Max resides in Montague, Massachusetts, where he is head of the local Harley Davidson Easy Rider's Club. He single-handedly illustrated this catalog. Way to go, Max.

Felix Bliss is a native of Santa Cruz, California, and is the founder of the Monterey Harmonica Orchestra. He is the author of three books, including the cult best-seller *Growing Up Cosmic*. An avid gardener and botanist, Felix lives with his wife, Kate, and their dog, Phred.

In Search of the New Age is a tremendous labor of love. We hope that you will enjoy the materials presented here, and that this catalog will stimulate, engage, and expand your mind. Used as a tool for exploration, this work may well change your life, as it has changed ours.

Healthfully,

Felix Bliss

Felix Bliss
Editor

In Search of the
New Age

Chapter

1

Services for an Enlightened Society

The mind boggles at the myriad of services spawned by the New Age. If your lifestyle's been evolving just a little bit faster than you can keep up with, then this guide to sensitive, professional help is just what you need. You'll find everything from attorneys specializing in unresolved past life disputes to seeing third-eye dogs for the psychically blind.

In order to give you a reliable evaluation of some of the more prominent New Age services, our staff has personally tried and tested each of the services listed in this directory. We can't predict which ones will work for you, but we can guarantee they'll all add to your expanding personal universe.

Talk with Dolphins in Their Native Tongue

IT IS PRESUMPTUOUS, if not foolhardy, to assume that dolphins understand only the English language. Yet judging by the work of hundreds of dolphin researchers during the past several decades, it seems to be a foregone conclusion that our frisky friends from the sea were raised on the King's English. But think about this for a moment. Dolphins come from a variety of geographical areas and climates. It's only logical that they should enjoy the same variety of language that humans do.

The Aquatic Language Society believes that not only are dolphins vastly more intelligent than humans, but they enjoy a command of a vast array of languages. Yes, it is true that a dolphin can readily learn English if that's the only language being spoken. But wouldn't it really be a lot more considerate to speak to a dolphin in its native tongue? The people at the Aquatic Language Society think so. With this in mind, they have developed a comprehensive learning program in dolphin languages.

Depending on where the dolphin at hand originates from, it may be communicating in Spanish, French, Italian, Greek, or any of a number of common languages. If you really want to communicate with dolphins, fluency in a variety of languages is indispensable.

Because dolphins are known to be telepathic, the Aquatic Language Society also offers training in trans-species psychic communication. This training includes remaining in the water with dolphins for several weeks at a time, under a pyramid specially charged with rare quartz crystals. The purported effect of this intensive experience is total psychic rapport with dolphins, and the ability to swim very quickly while balancing a ball on one's nose.

If you wish to develop your trans-species communication skills or to know more about the relationship between humans and sea mammals, you can dial toll-free 1-777-FSHTALK.

Reincarnation Life Insurance

Take the Fear out of Death

THE FOLKS AT Diamond Sutra Life & Casualty are sharper than a bunch of Roshis on Retreat. To take the fear out of death, they've come up with Reincarnation Life Insurance, a comprehensive, affordable insurance program that covers you and your family.

Let's face it. Most people aren't that afraid of being dead. The body stops, and that's the end of the show. It's what happens afterward that scares the bejesus out of most folks. After all, there's no way of telling whether you'll come back as a rich plantation owner in Texas or a starving beggar in Calcutta. If you ever need insurance, it will be at the time you drop your body and reincarnate.

Here's how Reincarnation Life Insurance works. You decide what future incarnation would be most desirable for you. You rank the incarnations you fear the most according to detailed incarnation value charts. Premiums are calculated by ranking that list against your likelihood of winding up with them, through a comprehensive aura reading. All these data are analyzed, along with the dollar amount of insurance you want. From all this, a fee schedule is determined. Should you return as a miserable poverty case, Diamond Sutra will put you back in the Gucci lane. Of course, if you desire to come back as a prince, and there is virtually zero possibility of that, your insurance payments will be hefty. If, however, you desire a reasonable afterlife— say as a Buick dealer in Paramus, New Jersey—your payments will be lower.

It's that simple. Unless you come back as a total mutant, Reincarnation Life Insurance is your ticket to a pleasant future.

REINCARNATION LIFE INSURANCE APPLICATION

Please fill out the following questionnaire completely. The answers given below, and the life choices you select, determine what your Reincarnation Life Insurance premiums will be. Thus it is important that you answer all questions fully and correctly.

1. Name _____

2. Address _____

3. City _____ State _____ Zip _____

4. Date of birth (this lifetime) _____ 5. Sex: Yes ___ No ___

6. If Yes, how frequently? If No, why not? _____

7. List your last THREE previous incarnations, last one first, including lifespan dates, places of birth, and causes of death for each. _____
_____
_____

8. Current occupation, and monthly rate of pay _____
_____

9. Religious or spiritual affiliations _____
_____

10. Your personal mantra (this will be kept confidential) _____
_____

11. Are there or have there ever been any shamans, mediums, or high incarnations in your family? _____

12. Do you have 20/20 Third Eye vision? _____

13. Are you a certified Lucid Dreamer? _____

14. Do you experience sudden blasts of intense heat up your spine?   Yes ___ No ___

15. Describe on a separate page, in as much detail as possible, the future (next) incarnation that you desire. _____

16. Describe, on a separate page, in as much detail as possible, the future (next) incarnations that you fear the most. _____

17. Are you a member of the Astral Projection Air Force Reserves? _____

18. Have you taken the Bodhisattva Vow? _____

19. Are there extraterrestrials in your lineage? _____

20. Have you ever been Pope? _____

21. Have you ever been the Dalai Lama? _____

22. Are you currently an active trance channel? _____

23. Do you play any of the following instruments: Japanese ceremonial gong, Tibetan yak skin barrel drum, bone horn, finger cymbals, sitar, Pan's pipes, or kalimba? _____

24. Within the past three years, have you eaten magic mushrooms? _____

SEND YOUR COMPLETED APPLICATION TO: Reincarnation Life Insurance, One Park St., Rochester, VT 05767, along with a processing fee of $12.50 to receive your personalized Reincarnation Life Insurance Policy.

Astral Projection Tours

IF YOU'RE THE average occult Joe off the street, you've probably read a dozen or more books on astral projection. If you've followed the directions in any of those publications, you're probably pretty good at popping out of your body and staring at yourself as you lie in bed. The truth is, there are only so many times that you can be entertained by that kind of thing. Then you're left standing around outside your body with your astral thumb up your ectoplasmic nose. Wouldn't it be great if you could put your ability to leave your body to some greater use than just lingering around your bedroom in the dark?

Now there's Astral Projection Tours, a unique outfit designed to get you to those far-out realms where the physical body just can't tread. Now when you pop out of your body, you can cruise to exciting places and meet unique beings. Out-of-Body Travel Agency offers individual or group tours to the forty-nine Buddhist Lokas, the seven hell realms, and the Palace of Shambhala, with excursion fares to the Aboriginal Dream Time and the Huna Heavenly Reward.

Instead of just reading about the healing temples of the ECK Masters or the etheric wanderings of Paul Brunton, now you too can jaunt off to Valhalla or dance at an authentic Akashic Record hop. Ever wonder where all the heroes go when they drop their bodies? You can find out on a special tour of the Between-Lifetimes Limbo Lands. On the special Holy Spaces tour, you can meet the great beings behind all major religions. Play billiards with Buddha, go skiing with Christ. And, with the Frequent Projector program, you can earn bonus travel points.

Just imagine setting off on a one-night or ten-day adventure, with no luggage at all (not even a toothbrush). Astral Projection Tours is definitely a progressive step in an otherwise dull astral projection marketplace. For further information, send away for a free brochure to Astral Projection Tours, 21234 Ectoplasm Blvd., San Francisco, CA 94118.

Seeing Third-Eye Dogs for the Psychically Blind

EVEN IF YOUR five senses are in fine working order, you may suffer from psychic blindness. This affliction inhibits the natural ability to pick up vibrations and to be intuitively perceptive. Those who are psychically blind cannot tell whether they are in the presence of a high spiritual being or a low-level warlock. Up until now, such individuals have been at an extreme disadvantage in society's rapidly developing spiritual scene. Now, however, there are Seeing Third-Eye Dogs for the Psychically Blind.

The Psychic Canine Center in Turlock, California, trains Seeing Third-Eye Dogs for use by thousands of psychically blind people every year. "We ship out about ten dogs every week," says Buster Cornea, director of the center. "After years of investigation, we've found that Chow Chows far and away make the best Seeing Third-Eye Dogs. They're amazingly perceptive."

At the Psychic Canine Center the psychically blind are trained to use their psychically sensitive Chow Chows to full advantage. According to Cornea, "The dogs communicate very well. When they're around someone sleazy, they growl in a low tone. When they are in the presence of a saint, their tails whack the heck out of the furniture." The psychic dogs can also vibe out places in moments. "Our dogs know right away if they're at a sacred burial site, or if there are poltergeists around. One of the worst things that the psychically blind can run into is poltergeist activity. They don't know how to interpret teacups flying through the air and that kind of thing."

Seeing Third-Eye Dogs make excellent companions, are well behaved, and live long lives. If you are psychically handicapped or know someone who is, you can obtain further information on Seeing Third-Eye Dogs by calling toll-free 1-777-VIBEDOG.

The Missing Soul Mates Bureau

EVERYONE LONGS TO find his or her soul mate. Yet the sad truth is that relatively few people actually find their true spiritual companion. Most of the time, we wind up with someone who is comfortable to be with, but isn't our one eternal partner. Up until now, there hasn't been much anyone could do about this, except perhaps to troop off to the Himalayas or some other remote part of the globe and get assistance from a sage.

But that sad state of affairs has been changed forever by the Missing Soul Mates Bureau. The Bureau assists individuals in reuniting with their soul mates through its *Lost Soul Journal.* For a modest fee you can place an ad in the journal to contact your long-lost loved one. The journal is given free to anyone who is searching, and circulation is substantial.

The following are typical entries:

Slim Asian Male, 33, seeks African beauty last seen in vicinity of Niger River Delta around 1750. You had a bone through your nose and a wide porcelain lip plate. Remember the oxen accident in the lentil fields? Respond to Box 158.

Sexy Parisian Female, 28, seeks Spanish bullfighter, circa 1870. Sorry I didn't wait for you. The last bull made quite a mess of you. Recall a garter full of gold coins and unforgettable nights behind the arena. Please answer. Box 73.

Though some ads go unanswered, many mateless souls have reunited with their partners thanks to the Missing Soul Mates Bureau. If you're missing your significant other, write to the Missing Soul Mates Bureau, 34 Firestorm Ave., Minot, ND.

Good Vibrations Cleaners

IS YOUR HOUSE loaded with vibes from the people who lived there before you? Is your work space so thick with leftover energy that your mood changes the moment you walk in the door? Does it feel as though the vibes in your environment are literally smeared all over the walls?

Let Good Vibrations Cleaners scrub clean the years of vibrational buildup in your house, office, or play environment. Good Vibrations Cleaners will rid any space of pesky leftover vibrations. They guarantee to get the job done, first time every time, or you pay nothing.

Good Vibrations Cleaners will come into your environment with sacred crystals, bowls full of cedar chips, and heavily perfumed joss sticks. Starting at one end of the space, they chant, burn the cedar chips and incense, and make sacred pentacles in the air with their crystals. As they do this, they send leftover vibes flying right out the open doors and windows. The service is concluded by sealing off your space from unwanted spirit intruders, thereby guaranteeing that the vibes in your environment are strictly of your own creation.

You need never again suffer from "leftover vibration syndrome," a complaint that bothers millions of helpless sufferers every day. Universal Vibe Cleaners has offices in all major urban areas. Franchises are available. For information, call toll-free 1-777-VIBEGON.

Beyond Firewalking: Huna Lava Surfing

SO YOU'VE FIREWALKED. That means that you scooted across a few hot coals, in less than two seconds. Such a backyard version of ancient Javanese fire dancing is a sad commentary on the commercialization of sacred rituals. If you truly want to challenge the very limits of your soul, lay your mortality on the line, and scream "Kowabunga," you were born for Huna Lava Surfing.

Huna Lava Surfing isn't some sort of three-day executive high-ropes course. With Huna Lava Surfing, one small mistake means that you've bought the farm. On the southern slope of the island of Hawaii lies Mauna Kea, an active volcano from which 3,000-degree molten lava pours day after day. As it cools, the lava runs in waves down steep tropical mountainsides. A Huna Lava Surfer rides these molten waves, on a specially designed titanium surfboard, at incredible speeds. One small slip of the foot, and the surfer melts into the lava forever. On the slopes, there are expert Hunas who have been surfing for decades. The secret of these spectacular athletes is a will developed over years and the coolness of mind to face death every day.

Perhaps you've been to a fearlessness workshop or taken some sort of training in how to be a warrior. Do you think you're ready for Huna Lava Surfing? If you really believe that you've walked on fire, then this terrifying sacred sport is for you. Old-time lava surfer Max Freedom Longboard describes the terror of riding lava. "The first time you look at it, you'll soil your shorts. Then you'll pass out. When you wake up, all you'll want to do is get out of there."

Most urban warriors, New Age shamans, channels, and gurus do in fact run away. Huna Lava Surfing is the ultimate test of one-pointedness.

To find out more about Huna Lava Surfing, show up at Mauna Kea any morning at sunrise and catch the waves.

Earth Changes Real Estate

IF YOU'RE AWARE of the prophecies of Nostradamus, the psychic readings of Edgar Cayce, or the voluminous teachings of Rambo-Tha, then you know that earth changes are on the way. This isn't a little rain or a particularly harsh winter we're talking about. If the prophets are correct, we are going to see the earth divide itself up suddenly and unexpectedly like a jigsaw puzzle run amok, and vibrate like a Magic Fingers mattress. Mountains will be valleys, oceans will be deserts, and rivers will swell to twenty times their size. Boogaloo down Broadway while all this is going on, and you may wind up in Toledo.

Earth Changes Real Estate offers a unique opportunity to cash in on the coming geophysical crisis in a big way. By compiling a vast array of predictions from various seers, psychics, and sages, Earth Changes Real Estate has pinpointed specific areas on Earth as sites for the next real estate bonanza. Earth Changes Real Estate offers beachfront property in Utah, Mississippi River Mountain house lots, and Atlantean condo communities—all at bargain-basement speculative rates.

Whoever would have thought that sleepy Billings, Montana, would be the next New York City? According to Edgar Cayce, that's exactly what's going to happen. But why wait for the sea to come crashing down your street? Earth Changes Real Estate offers Phase One prices on Montana condo properties right now. Or how about that Bermuda Triangle? If you think it's just the ocean's version of a black hole, won't you be surprised when the sacred temples of Atlantis come charging up out of the water, along with millions of acres of prime real estate!

Through Earth Changes Real Estate you can secure a deed for land that hasn't surfaced yet. Then, when the big tsunami comes rolling across your neighborhood, just hop into your Zodiac lifeboat and head for home. Don't let the Apocalypse ruin your garden party. You can cash in on the coming cataclysms, and start anew on prime property. Earth Changes Real Estate—turning disaster into opportunity. For free information, dial toll-free 1-777-NOEARTH.

Spiritual Names by Mail

IT CAN BE said that your name is your identity. But what if you choose to grow and evolve, and change that identity? It is often the case that people become increasingly spiritual, yet are still bogged down by their old names. Spiritual Names by Mail is a unique service designed to fit your name to your new, expanded sense of self. Spiritual Names by Mail is run by a group of genuine holy men who specialize in changing people's names to match their karma and their spiritual growth. These enlightened guys know that once you get your name right, your destiny train will switch to the fast track.

A case in point is that of Ralph Sedgewick of Dover, New Jersey. Ralph got into Transcendental Perspiration about three years ago, and his life really started to change. But everyone still knew him as Ralph, and he was stuck in that identity.

Thanks to Spiritual Names by Mail, he is now Shree Ralph Sedgewick Ananda and is now held in high esteem by his friends, family, and associates. "Having a new name is like being born again," states Shree Ralph. "I feel like I have a whole new life."

Murshid Alice Bagley Khan of Cottswold, England, agrees. "It's simply smashing, and very intriguing, to have a sufi spiritual name. I'm quite the talk at tea now."

Bhagwan Ben Schultz Ji of Butt, Wyoming, heartily endorses Spiritual Names by Mail. "Everybody treats me with a new sense of respect now that I have a spiritual name. Plus, it confuses the hell out of the phone company, which is always fun."

To put a little Maharishi in your moniker, send a recent photo of yourself and $200 to Spiritual Names by Mail, 657 Atomic Ave., Venice, CA 90291.

Rebirth Referral Service

WHAT CHANCE DOES a returning soul have of landing that really great paying job? Not much. At least, not until now. Rebirth Referral Service makes returning to the physical world easier. Now you can come back and move into a decent job, at a good salary, without having to "start at the bottom" for yet another lifetime.

How many times have you worked part-time odd jobs at a low wage? Maybe you were an assistant goat herd in Greece, a limestone quarry clean-up boy in Egypt, a pot washer in medieval Europe, a stall mucker in the wild West. If you're like most folks these days, you don't care to go through that again. Now you can start out your next life in a comfortable executive position.

Rebirth Referral Service offers a unique service for people in the work force who know they're going to return to this plane yet again. If you're a skilled professional in an executive or managerial position, you already qualify for reincarnation referral. How it works is simple. You sign up with the service and pay a one-time fee. There are no extra, hidden charges. When you die, our team of Tibetan lamas will track you to your next life. Once your location has been found, you'll be directed to an employer who has already pre-approved you.

Build your future security now. March into your next lifetime secure, confident—and employed. For information on Rebirth Referral, call toll-free 1-777-JOBLESS.

Karma Donors

KARMA DONORS IS a fantastic concept. By becoming a Karma Donor, you automatically leave behind a substantial amount of good or bad karma when you die.

It makes sense when you think about it. After all, people leave their kidneys, their hearts, even their eyes behind. Why not leave excess karma too?

Let's say you've got tons of bad karma. There's no question that something big is going to hit the fan the next time you incarnate. If you could just unload a bit of it, your next life would be easier. At the same time, this could be a tremendous boon to the recipient of your gift. After all, there are some people in the world who have accrued so much good karma, and so little bad karma, that their lives are a hell of smiling faces, "have a nice days," and "please 'n' thank yous." These folks could use a little friction to speed up their evolution.

On the other hand, let's say you've earned gobs of good karma. Don't you think that you could spare a little for some hapless bloke down on his luck for yet another lifetime? Your good Karma Donation could be just the thing he needs to get out of his evolutionary funk and stand tall and proud for a change.

By becoming a Karma Donor, you receive a wallet card that identifies you as a donor. That card is your way of saying that you care about the evolution of your fellow humans.

Think about it. Can't you spare a bit of your evolutionary baggage? For information on how you can become a Karma Donor, call toll-free 1-777-MYKARMA.

KARMA DONORS APPLICATION

To become a Karma Donor, you must answer the following questions. Once you have filled out this application, mail it to Karma Donors. Within six weeks, you will receive your Karma Donors Card, good for this lifetime. Upon the ascension of your spirit from your current mortal frame, your Karma donation will be made to a needy soul.

Name _____

Address _____

_____

Which do you wish to donate?   Good Karma ____   Bad Karma ____

Your Current Spiritual lineage.
____ 1. Buddist
____ 2. Christian
____ 3. Muslem
____ 4. Hindu
____ 5. Jain
____ 6. Jewish
____ 7. Shinto
____ 8. Tribal/Aboriginal
____ 9. Other

Name of your current Teacher/Advisor/Spirit Guide _____

Have you ever had a Certified Aura Reading? _____

If you have, please enclose a copy of the report. Enclosed _____

Have you made any binding agreements pertaining to your afterlife?
____ Yes
____ No

If so, what are they? _____

Have you ever taken the Bodhisattva Vow? _____

Please mail this form to Karma Donors, 423 Puscatoo Breezeway, Little Stag, WY 89862. Thank you for your Karma Donation!

Soul Mate Divorce

A FEW YEARS ago you met someone special. It was wonderful. Fireworks went off for both of you. You each remembered precious shared moments in past lives. Your sex was true tantric love. You both were in an exquisite, deliriously in-love condition. Psychics confirmed what you already knew intuitively. You indeed had found your soul mate.

It's years later, the glow is gone, the sex is ordinary, and your soul mate is a millstone around your neck. You rarely have fun anymore, and you wonder what the hell you're doing together. Your partner takes the biggest piece of cake, squeezes the toothpaste from the middle, and generally irks the daylights out of you. Face it—the relationship is dead.

Soul Mate Divorce is the latest service offered by divorce specialists Jacuzzi and Mire of New York. With Soul Mate Divorce you get a complete legal divorce, in keeping with your spiritual lifestyle. Through creative counseling, you and your soon-to-be ex-mate decide who gets the hot tub, the floatation tank, the Buddha in the meditation room, and the Oriental art in your condo. The whole process is designed to create as few karmic obligations as possible.

You and your partner will each be guided through creative separation visualizations, and each of you will receive your own personalized divorce mantra. Staff psychics will assist you both in resolving your disputes in this lifetime. After all, you'll probably wind up together again in another lifetime.

If your soul mate has turned out to be an albatross, Soul Mate Divorce may be the answer for you. For information, or to make an appointment with a certified Soul Mate Divorce lawyer, call toll-free 1-777-DIVORCE.

Hypocrite's Health Spa

HEALTH SPAS THAT STARVE and exercise you until you drop are a dime a dozen. Yet you may not wish to be pushed, pummeled, and badgered into a new, slimmer self. If what you want to exercise above all is *choice*, then Hypocrite's Health Spa is for you.

At Hypocrite's, you exercise the right to do exactly anything you please, and your diet is whatever you put into your mouth. The staff at Hypocrite's realizes that you are entitled to do whatever you like. After all, you are the customer. When you tell your friends and co-workers that you're going to a health spa for a week, they'll respect your high level of commitment to personal well-being. But your definition of well-being may be far afield from theirs. While they picture you running a ten-kilometer course every morning, you'll be zipping around nine easy holes in a golf cart. While they imagine you swimming fifty laps before lunch, you'll be on an inflatable raft with a drink in your hand. And while they envision you nibbling on watercress salad, you'll be slurping your way through prime rib of beef au jus, with all the trimmings. Why starve, when you can satisfy your hungers in a pleasing, relaxing environment?

Yes, this is just the place for *you* to relax! If you want the social benefits that come from appearing to be fitness-conscious but have more important things to do than work for them, the folks at Hypocrite's Health Spa will be happy to provide you with the facade of health respectability. Even if you come home from the spa weighing more than when you left, your friends will think it's simply a result of your improved muscle tone. After all, you were at a health spa!

For information on the Hypocrite's Health Spa nearest you, call toll-free 1-777-INDULGE.

The Center for Tongue Fu

DO YOU ENVY people with exceptional verbal skills? Are you thoroughly impressed by individuals who know how to deliver the most clever line possible at just the right moment? Are you awed by men and women who command the attention of any size group with their powerful communication skills?

If you answered yes to any of the above, you're not alone. Statistics show that most people are verbally inept, are infrequently clever, and shrivel when required to speak in front of a group. But there is hope. You can be the dynamic, commanding, inspiring speaker you've always wanted to be. The Center for Tongue Fu, in Button Hole, Wyoming, is now accepting a limited number of students every semester, to become certified Masters of Tongue Fu.

The intensive nine-month training at CTF is designed to turn you into a riveting speaker with hypnotic powers. You've heard the expression "sharp tongue"? How about "tongue lashing"? These colloquialisms refer to the mastery of tongue fu, an ancient art that can be used in any situation where verbal skills are required.

Let's say you're at a party. As a Master of Tongue Fu, you will be at the very center of activity, spinning tales, telling jokes, and being terribly clever. With your tongue fu skills, you'll be able to charm the pants right off anybody with just a casual turn of a phrase. On the other hand, in a confrontation or argument, you'll be able to tongue-lash others to a state of complete humiliation and embarassment. People will cower at the very thought of challenging you.

Tongue Fu can turn an average speaker into a verbal powerhouse. Consider the mastery of tongue fu to be like the keys to a city. With sensational verbal skills, you can go anywhere, have access to anything.

If you're ready to elevate yourself to heroic heights of communication, contact the Center for Tongue Fu, P.O. Box 475, Button Hole, WY 83025.

Death: Is It for You?

THROUGHOUT HUMAN HISTORY, not everyone has been eager to go to their eternal resting place. Truth be known, most people are pretty attached to their current incarnation and would like to extend their time on Earth. Sure, you'll reincarnate, but as who? Or what?

Take the uncertainty out of death with Body Futures, the new service that lets you decide which way to go, or not to go at all. Body Futures of Palo Alto, California, offers a complete selection of alternatives to dying, including the following.

Seal-A-Soul: In their state-of-the-art labs, Body Futures will flash-freeze you in 1/100th of a second and keep you in ultracold storage until the date or age of your choice. Then they'll thaw you out, and you can resume life in the exotic future.

Bionic Bod: Upon dropping your mortal frame, your brain will immediately be resuscitated and transplanted to the exciting new Eterna II bionic body, a fully operative titanium and latex bio frame that is virtually maintenance-free. The Eterna II comes in all sizes, in both sexes (or androgynous), and in a variety of ethnic and racial flavors. The Eterna II will give you generations of happy living pleasure.

Ben Pak: At the time of death, Body Futures will convert the essence of your soul into a holographic picture, which you can make appear and reappear at will. Then, at any time of day or night, you can appear to family members and friends and tell them in a mysterious tone of voice that the Force is with them.

Body Futures has changed the entire complexion of death today. The truth is, if you really don't want to go, you really don't have to. For further information on how you can extend your life, write to Body Futures, 666 Yeehah Drive, Palo Alto, CA 90296.

SECT-CHANGE OPERATIONS

As you evolve, so do your beliefs and interests. Sure, you may be a devoted Zen Buddhist today, but tomorrow you may be running around in orange pajamas chanting "Hare Krishna." And why not? Experimentation with a variety of religious and spiritual traditions can help you to develop a broader understanding than you could ever attain by staying in just one group.

TransSectuals is a group of cosmetic surgeons specializing in sect-change operations. TransSectuals offers a complete variety of cosmetic services, including radical and gradual sect changes. This unique service is designed to meet the needs of a rapidly evolving spiritual culture, a culture whose credo is change.

Here's how a sect-change operation works. Let's say you're a devout follower of Tibetan Buddhism. This means that you have short hair, are clean shaven, and have thick callused knees from thousands of devotional prostrations. But you've undergone an inner change, and you want to become a Hare Krishna. TransSectuals will remove the calluses from your knees and transplant them to your feet. This is because a seasoned Krishna devotee is on his feet dancing for hours every day. Next, if you're a man, you'll receive a hair transplant, a handsome eight-inch tassle on the back of your bald head. Last, you're given a smooth vertical groove carved in your forehead, as though you have been smearing sacred paste from your hairline to your nose for years. After the physical changes are complete, you undergo a three-day crash course in lingo and mannerisms of the sect you're going into. When this is complete, Presto! you've had a sect change.

For complete information, call Trans-Sectuals toll free at 1-777-CUTMEUP.

Extraterrestrial Abductees Support Group

LET'S SAY YOU have recently been abducted by extraterrestrials and then left off in the parking lot of a supermarket. If you're like most abductees, you probably don't know where to turn. Should you go to a psychic? Should you consult a priest? Should you blow your brains out? After all, being abducted by aliens from space can be a very disorienting experience.

The Extraterrestrial Abductees Support Group offers support and counseling for the ever-growing numbers of people who are suddenly snagged by delinquent E.T.'s. While such outrages used to be rare and occurred only in the dead of night in remote rural areas, abductions by aliens are now as common as BMWs and Cuisinarts. Now these kidnappings can occur anytime, anywhere. On your way to work, you may suddenly be whisked away for a three-day "brain-scrubbing" session, with Martians doing the cleaning. Try explaining that to the boss!

The worst part about being abducted is that you may not even remember what happened once you're returned to Earth. Take the case of Manuel Ramada of Chicopee, Massachusetts. While standing in his backyard, he was spirited away by a large spaceship, only to be returned several days later, with no recollection of what had happened during the interim period, and minus his AT&T Calling Card. "At first I thought I was watching another cloud of toxic gases from the Confederate Carbide factory," recalls Ramada. "Next thing I knew, I was surrounded by two-headed crocodiles wearing lab coats. It was weird."

Thanks to several intensive memory reconstruction sessions led by the Extraterrestrial Abductees Support Group, Manuel was able to remember what had happened to him, as well as several things that didn't, during the time he was missing. "There were five of these beings, and they all looked like Day-Glo gerbils. They stuck all sorts of probes into my body and made my head shake until my brain felt like a smoothie."

What are the telltale symptoms of having been abducted? If you've "lost" three or four days, if you went to the store to get milk and came back a week later (without the milk), or if you woke up to discover that it was next week, you may well have been abducted by aliens. Don't let a bunch of little jerks from another galaxy turn your mind into a Slurpee. Help is available at the push of a telephone button. Contact the Extraterrestrial Abductees Support Group. For information or someone to talk with, dial toll-free 1-777-MARTIAN.

45

Are You an Abductee?

HAVE YOU BEEN abducted by extraterrestrials? It is entirely possible that you have been, whether or not you remember it. The majority of abductees do not recall their encounters with beings from other galaxies, because abductions usually include "brain-scrubbing" sessions, leaving a blank space in the abductee's mind.

Thanks to advances in psychology and sophisticated techniques of hypnosis, many individuals are now able to recall their bizarre and frightening interactions with extraterrestrials. The following questionnaire has been designed in conjunction with top researchers in the field of extraterrestrial investigation. Please take time to answer all questions fully. In the process of filling out this questionnaire, you may begin to recall an abduction experience. There is every reason to suspect that thousands of people have unwittingly been abducted in the last decade.

1. Have you ever had either a single UFO or an entire Star Fleet Exploration Squadron land in your yard?
2. Do you recall meeting one or more blue-colored beings with narrow, bladelike heads?
3. Have you ever found yourself missing?
4. Have you ever "awoken" suddenly, in an entirely different place than where you were the last time you checked?
5. Are there unexplainable marks, bruises, or cuts on your body that you don't recall getting, like a tattoo on your fanny?
6. Does the name "Zolton the Intrepid" mean anything to you?
7. When you dream, do you imagine traveling in hyperspace?
8. Have you or your spouse given birth to a creature that your doctor can't identify?
9. Have you noticed an antenna growing out of the top of your head?
10. At mealtime, do you crave a large helping of dust?
11. At night, have you spotted beings who glow in the dark walking through your home?
12. Is one of your parents from a different planet?
13. Do you watch Star Trek reruns?
14. When you were a child, did your babysitter have a long, prehensile tail?
15. Is your waking body temperature below forty-three degrees?

If you answered yes to two or more of the above questions, the odds are excellent that you have in fact had a close encounter of the abduction kind. We recommend that you send your completed questionnaire to the Extraterrestrial Abductees Support Group, P.O. Box 934, OhMama, NB. May the Force be with you!

Chapter

2

Tuning In to Channeling

Channeling is a psychic process by which a being without a body assumes temporary control over someone, usually to communicate great teachings (and occasionally to give stock market advice). People who offer themselves as the vehicles for these messages are sometimes called "trance channelers," or just "channels" for short.

In the past few years a great deal has been said about channeling, and thousands of new channels and disembodied entities have burst upon the New Age scene. To separate the wheat from the chaff, our editors sat at the feet of literally hundreds of channelers and have selected the following few individuals as the creme de la creme of trance channels.

HOUSEWIFE LANE BOBS of Spud, Iowa, was hanging her laundry in the backyard when she had an extraordinary vision of a handsome old man speaking very quickly. This was her first introduction to Meth, the 100-mile-per-second speed-rapping entity whom she now channels. Meth claims to have been a nineteenth-century chemist and a pioneer in pharmacology in his last incarnation. His favorite expression is "Let me tell you about it real quick."

It is hard to tell why this entity is so wound up. Whatever the case may be, Meth is prolific, if nothing else. In a span of five short years, Meth has dictated over seventy-four books through Lane Bobs, and there appears to be no end to the flow. His seminal work is the great tome *The Nature of Personal, Professional, and Planetary Reality*. In this work Meth develops his theory that we all create our own reality, in any circumstance. "This has probably happened to you a million times," he proposes. "You're walking along thinking about a plate of tuna sushi, and someone comes up to you and says 'plate,' or 'sushi,' or 'plate of sushi.'"

As much as fifty percent of what Meth says would be lost in the eternal vapors if not for high-speed recording equipment, which captures his words as they fly by. Specially prepared tapes of *Meth Speaks*, which have been slowed down to one-third of their original speed, are available. For information and literature, call toll-free 1-777-METHRAP.

Rambo-Tha

THEY CALL HIM the Warrior, the Great One, the Invincible. Rambo-Tha, the entity who has taken the media by storm, claims to be a 35,000-year-old warrior sage from a pre-Sumerian civilization.

Rambo-Tha is channeled through Dazey Lite, a Seattle housewife who encountered the astral sage while sitting under a hair dryer in a beauty salon. As the Rambo (as he is affectionately called by devotees) later explained, the hair dryer set up a unique psycho-electrical charge which enabled Dazey Lite's aura to expand into a psychic cone. Rambo-Tha descended into this cone, bursting into Dazey's mind in a brilliant flash. Rambo-Tha is far and away the best-known of all spirit teachers. Dazey holds regular seminars throughout the United States, where for $500 you can sit for a weekend at the feet of the Rambo.

When Rambo-Tha overtakes Dazey Lite's small but well-proportioned body, she begins to stamp her feet, furrow her brow, pucker her lips, and flare her nostrils. As the warrior aspect transforms her, she tosses her blond hair wildly about and announces in a booming voice, "I am the Rambo!"

Rambo-Tha works with devotees on what he refers to as "issues about prosperity." Operating on the theory that money sitting in the bank is really blocked energy, the Rambo encourages followers to get their financial juices flowing by circulating their money energy—to him. Dazey Lite is perk and chipper about the whole affair. "It's such an honor to be a humble servant of a God-enlightened soul like the Rambo," she squeals, her nipples tightening visibly under her sheer cashmere sweater as she counts the day's take.

For further information on the seminars and teachings of Rambo-Tha, call toll-free 1-777-CASHNOW.

Sister Cecilia

PERHAPS THE ODDEST case of all the trance channels we have encountered is that of Sister Cecilia, an eleventh-century prostitute who is channeled through Burl Fenster, a Montana lumberjack. "This is some really weird shit," admits Fenster, who first encountered the entity in a dream. Sister Cecilia's first public appearance happened in a small countryside bar. "I guess I just went into a trance," explains Fenster. "I came to on the bar stool, and everybody in the whole place was staring at me with these bizarre looks on their faces. I didn't know what had happened."

What had happened was that Sister Cecilia had given her first group talk. But this entity, unlike most others, offers no spiritual advice. Sister Cecilia is still soliciting. Some of her favorite quotes are "Come play in the warm, fertile fields of my tumescent mound" and "Wouldst thou care to lick the luscious lips of my loins?"

You can imagine the pain and embarrassment that this has caused Fenster, age 38, who spends his entire day around burly, muscular men. "I have no control over when she comes through. I've been punched out three times, and I don't even remember for what."

Sister Cecilia speaks in a sensuous, seductive voice, totally different from that of Fenster, whose normal speech is gruff and low. During our interview, Fenster lapsed into a spontaneous trance, and Sister Cecilia came through. "Come light upon my fleshy saddle," she invited "and ride me, ride me, ride me!" Despite the enthusiastic invitation, this editor declined.

TV Ananda

LIKE WOW! This entity is totally—really totally—far out! TV Ananda is a recently discovered entity channeled through Irma Schultz of Perth Amboy, New Jersey. After watching a television in a darkened living room for over thirty-four years, Schultz was contacted by TV Ananda, who appeared to her during a commercial break in *Lifestyles of the Rich and Famous.*

"At first I thought it was one of those special contests or some unusual promotional gimmick," explains Schultz, 57. "I never experienced anything like it. I thought maybe I won the lottery or woke up the ghost of Elvis." It was neither. It was a boob-tube junkie from the Great Beyond.

TV Ananda, who makes absolutely no claims to spiritual power, is a veritable lexicon of television lore. This entity can recite verbatim entire segments of *Mr. Ed, Leave It to Beaver, Dennis the Menace, Dragnet, Amos & Andy, Dobie Gillis, Pete and Gladys,* and *Topper.*

TV Ananda also recites entire commercials, from "Plop, plop, fizz, fizz, oh what a relief it is" to "Oh, I wish I were an Oscar Mayer wiener." He also can hum or whistle the theme song to over four hundred television programs, including the original *Wagon Train* (with Ward Bond).

TV Ananda offers no seminars, and Irma Schultz accepts no money for trance sessions. "Would you pay to listen to reruns?" she asks.

LAVORIS IS CHANNELED through Jack Putz, a former Los Angeles insurance salesman who awoke one night to an eerie glow illuminating his Beverly Hills bedroom. "At first I thought it was the neon sign from the Fat Burger stand on the corner," recalls Putz, 39, who is still somewhat baffled by his new occupation as a channeler. "But the Fat Burger sign is red, and the eerie glow in my bedroom was green." As Putz sat up in bed, a loud voice filled his head. It was Lavoris.

Lavoris claims never to have had a body. "I have not been fettered by the bonds of the flesh. I have always soared like an eagle above the teeming masses of humanity," he preaches. Lavoris, who refers to himself as the "divine breath," says that he exists "to bring a small patch of light into the cavernous shattered souls of groveling peoplehood."

When Putz holds weekend seminars with Lavoris, the room is packed with the well-heeled and well-known of Hollywood. Jane Fondle, a regular attendee, quips, "It's like an aerobic workout for the soul." Lavoris specializes in unorthodox healing techniques, and his followers are enthusiastic about the results. Recalls one bedazzled devotee, "I was terribly congested and was having trouble breathing. Lavoris told me to jam my pinkie way up my nostrils and ream them out. I followed his instructions, and my breathing improved instantly. He's just so incredibly tuned in." Other admirers claim to have been cured of hemorrhoids, acne, and chronic constipation, all by similar methods.

A full schedule of Lavoris appearances is available through the Lavoris Center in Los Angeles. For information on workshops in your area, dial toll-free 1-777-YOUPUTZ.

Chapter

3

On the Spiritual Path

The spiritual path can be a tricky, rocky road with temptations at every turn. In the interest of helping all sincere truth seekers to travel that path, we have assembled a list of some of the most reliable (if unorthodox) spiritual aids and resources. Use them freely!

Tanning Secrets of the Yogis

HAVE YOU EVER noticed that all yogis have great tans? It's true. The yogis of all times have had deep, dark, fabulous tans. How do they do it? At the Hindu Tush Tanning Center in India, experts explain that the Yogic Tan is the tan to which all true sun worshipers aspire. "It is not enough to go out in the sun and lie around," explains Ananda Soleil, director of the Tanning Center. "The first trick is that you must stay out almost all the time, mostly with nothing on but a loincloth." A Yogic Tan is achieved through years of eating, working, and just plain hanging out in the sun, almost naked, says Soleil.

The second trick is massage. Using a mixture of sandalwood oil and garbanzo bean paste, the yogis impart a dark luster to their bodies. The oil mixes with the dark film in their pores, and the effect is a dark brown polish over the entire body.

The third trick, says Soleil, is that when the yogis do wear clothing, it is made of white cotton. "This contrasts quite nicely with their color." The Hindu Tush Tanning Center offers intensive residential tanning programs all year long, except during monsoon season. To master the tanning methods presented at the center, a minimum stay of 120 days is recommended. For further information on the center, and a fee schedule, dial toll-free in the U.S. 1-777-YOGITAN.

New Age Mantras

EVERY ANCIENT SPIRITUAL tradition has its mantras, or words of power. A mantra is a word or phrase which, when intoned, empowers the one who utters it. Mantras can be found at the very heart of the Hindu tradition, but are not unique to the East. The "Amen" of the Christian faith is akin to the "OM" of the Hindus. Both mantras mean the One God, or the All and the Everything.

Wasn't there a time when mantras were new? Aren't there in fact mantras for today's needs? The answer to both questions is yes. New Age Mantras is an organization founded by the legendary Swami Snatchadollah. The primary function of the group is to serve humanity by providing mantras for a changing world. From their aerie in the Catskills, Swami Snatchadollah and his devotees have cranked out a whole new generation of words of power, including Om Condo Om, Sheik Yerkundalini Shakti, and Yes Condom Yes. New Age Mantras offers classes and workshops at their center and produces publications, including *The Word*, a quarterly journal. They also offer their popular workshop, "Creative Verbalization," all over the United States and in several European cities.

At the core of the teachings of Swami Snatchadollah is the New Age Maha Mantra. According to the swami, every age has a Maha Mantra, or great word of power. Drawing upon the vast tradition of Tibetan Buddhism, the Swami has divined the Maha Mantra of this age, OH MONEY PAD MY HOME. Constant repetition of this mantra is an invocation of fabulous spiritual and worldly riches, says Snatchadollah.

New Age Mantras also offers a rags-to-riches prosperity training, by correspondence. For information, call 1-777-BIGWORD.

Pray-for-Safety Interstate Worship Centers

WHAT DO YOU do when you want to worship while you travel? Pray-for-Safety Interstate Worship Centers offer road-weary travelers the opportunity to commune with their God of choice and to contribute to highway safety at the very same time.

Found all across the United States on interstate highways, Pray-for-Safety Interstate Worship Centers provide drive-in bays for the traveling churchgoers. Each bay is equipped with coin-operated church programs of all denominations, from Catholicism to Buddhism, including some obscure Shinto and Pali services. Drop a few coins into the donation slot, attach a window speaker to your car, roll down your window visor prayer shade, and commune with on high.

Pray-for-Safety Interstate Worship Centers have been shown to improve highway safety. Reverent drivers are safer drivers, are considerate on the road, drive within the speed limit, and help other travelers in distress. All this adds up to safer roadways and a more wholesome atmosphere on our interstate highway system.

The centers also carry a full selection of religious paraphernalia, available in vending machines. From Hindu incense car deodorizers to stick shift crosses made of sturdy, multicolored styrene plastic, there is something for everyone. And you can drive home the message of safety with their bumper stickers, including "Seat Belts or Satan" and "Lock Up—It's the Lord's Law."

Since cleanliness is next to godliness, Pray-for-Safety Interstate Worship Centers also offer self-service car wash facilities right in the worship bays. This means you can roll in, worship, wash your car, and drive off feeling and looking shiny and new.

The Chakra Training

ACCORDING TO THE traditional Hindu yogic scheme, there are energy vortices in the human body known as chakras. The seven chakras are considered to be the major centers of energy within each human being. These centers are related to glands, organs, and nerves in the physical body. They are also related to mental, emotional, and spiritual states of consciousness.

The Chakra Training is a workshop conducted by Walla Walla Bing Bang, a renunciate monk and yogi from the remote Himalayas. Recognizing the need to bring knowledge of the chakras to a spiritually inquisitive society, Bing Bang left his small hut in India to travel and teach in the United States. He has designed an eight-day residential training that thoroughly examines the chakras and the entire human energy system.

The following chart, designed by Walla Walla Bing Bang himself, shows the location of the chakras, describes their functions, and explains how the chakras are explored in The Chakra Training:

The Sex Chakra: The sex chakra is the home of lustful urges and libidinal surges. In learning the potential of this energy vortex, the student is led through a variety of Tantric Yoga practices, including pelvic thrusts and the ancient ring dang doo.

The Wallet Chakra: It is the contents, not the size, of one's wallet that determine its force. The wallet is the key to social power. A slim, gold-card-filled wallet is a passport to superior purchasing karma.

Food Chakra: This is the location of appetite, of the hungers and thirsts of the human spirit. Students are encouraged to discover their own unique sustenance, with the careful guidance of Bing Bang, who concludes each day's teachings with a trip to a different ethnic restaurant. Thai, Mexican, Japanese, Italian, Ethiopian, Chinese, Brazilian, and French foods are carefully studied during the course.

Chest Chakra: Truly, throughout the entire primate kingdom, the prominence of the chest is critical to the individual's position in the group order. For men, a broad, solid muscular chest represents inner strength and physical power. For women, pert, firm, well-formed breasts are at once captivating and commanding. Through the regular practice of pushups, isometrics, and parts of the original Charles Atlas fitness regime, the student learns to develop a comely and authoritative chest.

Mouth Chakra: This simple orifice with the primitive muscular ring is a treasure trove of words, articulations, and sounds for all occasions. Walla Walla Bing Bang is a renowned master of the mouth chakra. With his usual deftness, he explores whistling, blowing, puckering, and clucking. "A master of the mouth chakra," he says, "is like a small child wailing in the night. He can awaken anyone."

Eye Chakra: Truly the bay windows of the soul, mysterious, cool, well-focused eyes give the appearance of great inner power and mystique. They are also the rivets that fasten any business deal. In

The Chakra Training, students learn to cultivate "wise eyes." This look is particularly beneficial to religious and spiritual figures who must appear aloof and compassionately condescending.

Hair Chakra: Short, long, curly, stray, thick, thin, or partly gray—hair says a lot about who we are. It is the actual crown of the body, and is the height of fashion. Walla Walla, who himself sports thick, silver, sagely locks, examines the full potential of the hair chakra. Assistance in this part of the training is provided by Jean Claude Phillipe Fufu, noted stylist and aesthetician, whose specialty is the beehive coiffure shaped like Mount Kailash. Toupées, transplants, and hair weaving are also covered.

The Chakra Training is held in major urban areas nationwide. For a schedule of workshop dates and locations, contact Walla Walla Bing Bang, 42103 Puddle Street, Cambridge, MA 02139.

Tibetan Boozism: Out on a Binge

AT THE HEART of Tibetan culture is chang, a potent barley beer unlike any other brew in the world. Not only is chang an inebriate's delight; it also produces visions. It is chang which is at the heart of Tibetan Boozism, the monastic spiritual culture of Tibet.

While Tibetan Boozism is often confused with the Buddhist religion of India, the two could not be further apart. For while Buddhism requires strict discipline and austerity, Tibetan Boozism offers broad opportunity for wild abandon. Many is the winter night that you can hear the monks of the Boozist citadels banging bells, blowing horns, riding their frightened yaks through the hallways, whooping, and singing their bawdy Tibetan drinking songs.

But there is more to Boozist activities than just an endless, careening party. The visions produced by drinking chang are interpreted by temple seers, themselves serious juice heads, who use the visions to divine the future. Such "alcohoracles" drink their chang from huge brass mugs engraved with bulls and hockey players. So far their predictions have been completely inaccurate, but they keep imbibing in hopes of refining their insights.

Today Tibetan Boozism has spread to the Western world, thanks to the work of the heavy-drinking Lama Drunkpa Ricochet. The main Boozist center is in Topeka, Kansas. There thousands of students participate in sacred Boozist toga parties, decorate the Boozist center with rolls of sacred facial tissue, and drive a procession of Iroc-Z's through the center of town at high speed, in homage to the gods of the night. It is clear, as many of Ricochet's students loudly proclaim during their sacred parades: This Bhud's for you, America.

If you would like more information about Tibetan Boozism or about the teachings of Drunkpa Ricochet, call toll-free 1-777-DRUNKPA.

The Secret of the Great Pyramid

THE GREAT PYRAMID of Khufu, or Cheops, covers a sprawling thirteen acres at Gizeh, near Cairo. Built around 2680 B.C. along with two smaller pyramids, the Great Pyramid is one of the Seven Wonders of the World and is the spiritual focal spot for hundreds of arcane mystery schools. This massive structure, which can be seen from a distance of a hundred miles, is used to help navigate across the Egyptian desert. But why was it built? What purpose does it serve? Even more intriguing, will it go condo?

Archaeologist Peter Tombkins has exhaustively explored the Great Pyramid, its lore, and its secrets. What he has discovered is so far-reaching, so earth-shattering, that it virtually rewrites a thousand history books overnight. No, the pyramid wasn't constructed by extraterrestrials with superpowerful lasers. No, it wasn't made by some superhuman civilization that subsequently disappeared off the face of the earth. The truth is that the Great Pyramid of Khufu is actually the Great Pyramid of Tofu.

Around 3000 B.C., the entire Nile River Delta was a massive soybean field, the largest in history. Covering a vast expanse, the field produced bumper crops of soybeans, year after year, for generations. The Egyptians never did recognize these beans as food, but did use them in bean-shooter battles with the Assyrians. Around 2800 B.C., a traveling group of Macrobiotics from the primitive islands of Japan came upon the field of soybeans and were thoroughly awed. To these people, the soybean was the most precious jewel of creation. They immediately recognized the fertile bean field as a generous act of God. To honor the Deity, they decided to erect a monument made entirely of soybean curd.

And so it came to be that over a period of almost twenty years, the Macrobiotics led a team of 10,000 Canaanites, Hashemites, and assorted biblical tribespeople, who raked 160 square miles of soybean fields and gathered their harvest into great, square holding tanks by the banks of the Nile. When the mighty river flooded its banks, the beans were inundated in a rich silt which, under the action of the burning desert sun, cooked them until they began to release their precious milk. Then did the 20,000 feet of the assembled tribespeople press the beans like grapes, until their milk and the water had become as one. The river's own mineral salts congealed the milk into huge blocks of curd, which, when further dried under the rays of the solar disk, were cut into cubes of the proper size. These soybean blocks were easily carried by the tribespeople across the sands and put into their predetermined places, under the supervision of Pharaoh's architects. (Now, thanks to Professor Tombkin's research, the mystery of how the great pyramid's building blocks were transported is at last solved!) Once each piece of the monument was in place, the Priests of Ra initiated a still-secret process of alchemical petrification in which the sacred bean curd was transmuted into solid stone masses, making the Great Pyramid of Tofu.

Since the curing of the beans in the Great Pyramid of Tofu, droughts destroyed the soybeans fields, and today the Nile River Delta contains a vast expanse of desert near Cairo. The Great Pyramid of Tofu and the two smaller pyramids rest in the center of the desert as eternal reminders of a period of extraordinary fertility in the distant past of exotic Egypt.

A Course In Minutia
Developing Your Own Little Picture

Truth be known, the little things in life are virtually ignored by most spiritual traditions. Sure, there is occasionally some scriptural reference to "the beauty in a blade of grass," or some such. But can you think of any spiritual tradition whose members actually do contemplate the really simple things in life, like the warranty on a toothbrush? There are none.

Until now. Just in time, there is A Course in Minutia, a spiritual path in book form that explores the small side of life, in exacting detail. A Course in Minutia is written by an anonymous group of enlightened souls, formerly employed as proofreaders of dictionaries, who achieved their God-realized state through lifetimes of contemplating the number of dust mites in the lint of their navels. Once they came together in a higher realm, these sages recognized the need to expound upon and codify their unique path to self-realization. Thus, A Course in Minutia was born.

While many paths concentrate on the macrocosm, A Course in Minutia drops your attention down to the infinitely small. So leave the big picture to others. For more information on how you can develop your own little picture, call **A Course in Minutia** toll-free at **1-777-MINUTIA.**

Chapter

4

Who's Who in the New Age

You may have seen them in a dream, or perhaps on cable TV. They are the most powerful beings in the New Age: the spiritual teachers. Visionaries devoted to realizing the highest in human potential, these people have reincarnated for the sole purpose of helping the rest of us attain Nirvana. Like beacons of light, they show the way through dark and troubled times.

The following profiles of famous teachers may save you lifetimes of wandering and searching for the master who's right for you.

Reverend Flung Dung Loon and the Loonies

AS A YOUNG boy in his native Korean village of Sinanju, Flung Dung Loon was an avid gardener. One day while working in his backyard, Loon had a vision of Christ. In the vision he saw Jesus at a cash register, ringing up one sale after another as a procession of lost souls filed past him into the Kingdom of Heaven. This haunting vision transformed the mind of little Flung Dung, who realized at once that it was his destiny to be the Messiah, to lead humanity past the cash registers of eternity into the Kingdom of Heaven.

Only a few years later, Flung Dung launched the humble beginnings of the Loonification Church, which today is a sprawling multimillion-dollar church and corporate conglomerate, with subsidiaries in virtually all developed nations. "God is our business, and business is our God" is the credo of the Loonies, whose businesses include several fishing fleets, newspapers, munitions manufacturing, beverage bottling, a ginseng products company, and an international network of florists.

Loon, who recently finished a stint at prison for income tax fraud, describes himself as "a humble soul who is the one and only chosen of God." His privileged followers work long hours for no pay, dissociate themselves from all family and friends, and vow loyalty to Loon to the death. Upper management opportunities in the Loonification Church are relatively rare, but such positions offer excellent training in both reality distortion and mind control. For further information on Flung Dung and the Loonies, find a flower vendor on the street and strike up a conversation. You'll be sorry you did.

The Teachings of Long John

A Yankee Way of Knowledge
by Charlie Castanettes

EDITOR'S NOTE: Since his first published work in 1969, Charlie Castanettes has explored the world of the shaman and has uncovered the secrets of an age-old wisdom tradition. In his two past works, *Wheels of Power* and *The Tao of Speeding*, Castanettes penetrated further into the knowledge of his mentor, Long John, a highly expert master of the road. Now, in his latest book, *The Teachings of Long John: A Yankee Way of Knowledge*, Castanettes recounts his extraordinary journey along the highways of life as Long John's apprentice. *In Search of the New Age* is pleased to present the first chapter of Charlie Castanettes' new book, in advance of its publication. *The Teachings of Long John* will be available in hardback early next year.

"I understand that you are a master of the road," I said to the old man in front of me.

We were standing in a restaurant at a truck stop on Interstate 95 in Connecticut. A friend had introduced us and then had departed to the men's room, giving us a chance to talk. The old man had said that his name was Long John Mateus.

"Your friend said that?" he queried.

"Well, yes."

"Let's just say that the road and I have a certain understanding. I don't just drive it. Rather, we are extensions of each other. You understand?"

I told him that I didn't, but that I hoped we could get together for a meaningful dialogue on the subject.

"Meaningful dialogue?" he asked incredulously. "What are you, from Marin County or something? You don't have a meaningful dialogue about the road. You either drive it or you don't."

His eyes penetrated deeply into mine. I began to sweat and felt a painful churning sensation in my abdomen. My subjective perception at the time was that Long John was "doing" something to me.

"Could we get together sometime," I faltered, "so that I could learn some of your knowledge of the road?"

Long John broke into a warm smile, and at once the sensations in my abdomen ceased.

"Sure," he said. Then, squinting, as if he were looking around me, not at me, he added, "If you qualify, I may even teach you the Tao of Speeding. You're a writer, correct?"

I acknowledged that I was. "But how did you know?"

"The Smith Corona portable typewriter on your table gave you away. Who knows, you may even be able to make some money out of this whole deal."

I assured Long John that I was not at all concerned with material gain.

"Oh, wonderful, then," he replied, breaking into a loud laugh. "You can sign over all your royalties to me. I still have to put food on the table." He laughed some more and then slapped me on the back very hard, as though I had just told him the greatest of jokes. I felt like a fool. Then, reaching into his front shirt pocket, he produced a card. "Here's my business phone. Leave a message on my answering machine, and I'll get back to you."

He nodded his head courteously, and strode out the doors of the restaurant to a black Trans Am. I walked out to watch him go and stood under the gas plaza. He pulled up beside me and rolled down his car window. "We must now be like the smell of gasoline," he said. "Maybe it'll get into your nose again someday."

The Harvey Kirschman Story

Portrait of a Master

PERHAPS YOU'VE SEEN them in bus stations, airports, and city parks. Recognizable by their shaved heads (except for a tassle in back), flowing orange robes, and hi-top sneakers, the Harvey Kirschmans can usually be found clanging cymbals, pounding drums, and dancing up a storm as they incessantly intone the name of their founder and spiritual guide.

> Harvey Kirschman, Harvey Kirschman, Kirschman Kirschman, Harvey Harvey.

Harvard G. Kirschman was born to a poor but loving Jewish family on Coney Island during the Roaring Twenties. Though he worked by day in his father's bakery, Harvey's true love was music. With money he had scraped together from a full year of work, Harvey purchased his first pair of bongo drums at age 14.

Through his teens and into his early twenties, Harvey purchased a variety of hand drums, including congas, tambourines, and a large Tibetan yak skin barrel drum, which he came across in Manhattan. Though he dreamed of working as a percussionist, Harvey was bound to the family business and eventually assumed the operation of the bakery.

Fate ordained that Harvey Kirschman's life would change radically during the summer of 1967. Harvey was in his early forties then, running the bakery and practicing percussion at night. He was somewhat portly (an occupational hazard) and completely bald except for one small patch of hair on the back of his head. It was the Summer of Love, the beginning of the hippie movement, and Harvey's teenage son, Rudi, was experimenting with LSD. Rudi was so enamored of the mind-expanding drug that he put some in his father's coffee one morning, before Harvey went off to work.

At the bakery, jelly doughnuts became flying saucers, crullers became submarines, whipped cream became the ocean, and sugar was a snowstorm. At opening time that morning, Harvey was found on his hands and knees on the bakery floor, creating a topographical map of Long Island with a frosting gun. He was taken home, put into his favorite orange bathrobe, and put to bed.

But Harvey's universe was expanding rapidly that day, and bed could not contain him. In his bathrobe and slippers, muttering his own name repeatedly, Harvey grabbed his Tibetan yak skin barrel drum and headed for a Love-In at Central Park.

At the Love-In, Harvey wandered around and pounded on his drum. Impressionable teenagers on LSD fell in behind him, echoing his chant and banging Popsicle sticks on Coke bottles.

Harvey never did come down from his LSD trip. He was deified by his followers, who now wear orange robes and shaved heads as a tribute to their leader. The Harvey Kirschman group is prominent in Detroit, Los Angeles, Chicago, and Boston, where they operate a chain of bakeries.

Swami Koolbanana (Joey Bananas)

CLEAN WITH SWAMI KOOLBANANA

Now is a once-in-a-lifetime opportunity to clean with the Master Janitor of the ages, Swami Koolbanana. Scrub away eons of karmic dross during hands-on cleaning workshops with the king of cleanup men. Swami Koolbanana is the absolute incarnation of cleaning prowess.

12,000–11,050 B.C.	Cleaned Animal Cages, Noah's Ark
20 B.C.–A.D. 40	Head Dishwasher, Bethlehem Inn
1502–1590	Head Janitor of Zen Center, Kyoto, Japan
1750–1830	Founder of Lama Laundry Service, Tibet
1945–	Self-Employed Soul Cleaner. Director of Clean Soul Centers, Hoboken, N.J., and Chelsea, Mass.

Hoboken, 3:00 A.M.	Chelsea, 2:00 A.M.
Mon., Nov. 8—$500	Thurs., Nov. 4—$500
Mon., Nov. 15—$500	Thurs., Nov. 11—$500
Mon., Nov. 22—$2,500 (Intensive)	Thurs., Nov. 18—$2,500 (Intensive)
Location: Kitchen, Holiday Inn	Location: Men's Room, Mike's Donut Shop
Hoboken, New Jersey	Chelsea, Massachusetts

"OM IS WHERE THE GERMS AIN'T!"—Swami Koolbanana

Bagman Shree Rag-Knees

WHAT CAN BE said about a 55-year-old self-taught Indian holy man who has authored over one hundred books, advocates the liberal use of sex and drugs, and has been thrown out of several Western countries? They don't come more controversial than Bagman Shree Rag-Knees.

In 1953 the Bagman was a small-time religion teacher in rural Northwest India. One night, while employing the services of a high-caste hooker, Bagman became enlightened. The details of the blessed event are sketchy, but the police report mentions the seizure of a tub of warm yogurt, a hysterical water buffalo, and copious amounts of Nepalese hashish. As the 21-year-old professor was having his flute played, he heard the celestial music all about him. Then, with a shudder, the mighty Kundalini shot up his spine, surging in waves. The fiery salvo eventually subsided, and the Bagman was bathed in the Divine Nectar.

Such a prestigious enlightenment carries with it heavy karmic duty. But the ever-studious Bagman rose to the task and began at once to pontificate on a broad range of religious and philosophical issues. With dispatch he answered the age-old questions that have tormented the world's greatest thinkers:

Q: What is the meaning of Life?
Bagman: There isn't any.

Q: Does God exist?
Bagman: Of course. But don't claim him as a credit reference.

Q: Why is there suffering?

Bagman: Tight underwear and high heels. Boxer shorts and sandals would solve many problems.

Such electrifying mental clarity has launched Bagman into the heavenly spotlight. Within several months after his enlightenment, Shree Rag-Knees started a communal center in Bombay. Today the camp is overflowing with devotees from all nations, who flock to hear the Bagman's critical discourses. "He is like a delicate lotus blossom on the rushing stream of life." Another devotee observed, "His words are like toast which has been burned in a red hot oven. They smoke and smolder and get in your eyes and choke you up."

The community in Bombay has grown as thousands of devotees have come to take part in the new, innovative psychotherapies which are "awakening" in the center. Such new methods include cooking, cleaning, building renovation, sewing, printing, and field work. Each of the therapies has its own exquisitely unique purpose. Cooking, for example, heats the inner juices of the personality, while building renovation helps the devotee to construct a spiritual identity.

At one shaky period in the development of the center, the Bagman was forced to sell some of his 130 Rolls-Royces to generate cash for food and supplies. "They have had one owner, and the mileage is low," he noted.

Today Bagman is back in full swing, giving daily discourse and running a lucrative worldwide fellowship of devotees. As he casually notes, "That's the biz, sweetheart."

Da Free Loo

NOW HERE IS a spiritual master with his feet planted firmly on the ground. While many masters give discourse on the subtleties of mantras, Da Free Loo has plunged into the main pipelines of society. His mission in the world is to end the tyranny of pay toilets. On this quest, Da Free Loo has tirelessly traveled from one nation to another, "to wipe out the hypocrisy of pay toilets, to flush out this evil from society."

As a boy, Da Free Loo was a student of the great Bowel of Bombay. It was at the feet of his master that Da embarked upon the path of his life mission. Today he is the leader of the Defecation Liberation Movement. As Da Free Loo himself describes it, "It is a huge movement. It is very satisfying." In the past several years, he and his followers have systematically purged over 200,000 pay toilets from over a dozen nations. "We will not cease our toil until we have blasted every pay toilet from the face of the earth," states Loo firmly.

Da believes that individuals should be able to relieve themselves without paying a fee. "It is a function of nature. You pay to own a home, you pay for food, you even pay to park your car. You should be able to answer the daily calls of nature for free." With this belief firmly in mind, he and his followers use crowbars to pry the doors off pay toilets and dispense the change from coin slots to the poor. "Everybody leaves a steaming heap," explains Da philosophically. "It is beyond class, beyond economics. My motto is 'Go in peace.'"

For further information on the Defecation Liberation Movement, call toll-free 1-777-FREEPOO.

Wormer Airhead and the
Airhead Seminar Training (AST)

WHEN JACK ROSEBAUM was a small child, he dreamed of growing up. He didn't want to be anything in particular. His main preoccupation was to get attention. As little Jack saw it, the world was filled with audience enough. But in his little world of suburban Passaic, New Jersey, Rosebaum seemed to be playing to an empty house.

In school he tried glee club, theater, and sports, all for attention. During lunch break he would position himself at the most visible spot in the cafeteria and eat standing up, just to be noticed. A few classmates would giggle at him, but for the most part he went through his day without notice. College was more of the same, plus hanging out in the student lounge, nattily dressed and scrubbed.

After college, Jack Rosebaum began to sell used cars. He also married. Within two years the happy couple had two children, and Jack had more attention than ever before.

On the used-car lot, Rosebaum would talk with customers and attempt to share his thoughts with them. "Don't you think you should take personal responsibility for this '57 Buick?" he would ask. "Isn't it synchronous that I sell used cars, and you're looking for one, and we've met, right here, in a used-car lot?" Customers would nod their heads or sometimes just stare.

Believing that he was destined for bigger things in life, Rosebaum stepped out for a loaf of bread one foggy November evening and disappeared, leaving his wife

and children to fend for themselves. Jack Rosebaum changed his name to Wormer Airhead and hit the road in his Plymouth Duster.

Over the next two years Airhead traveled from one city to another, attending as many encounter groups, ashrams, transpersonal workshops, and lectures on philosophy as he could find. At the end of that time he knew his destiny: he would become one of the gurus of the new personal growth movement. At last he would have the attention he so richly deserved. Throngs would sit at his feet, and his words would be like manna to them.

In 1972, Wormer Airhead held the first AST (Airhead Seminar Training) program. It was a modest financial success. But as far as attention was concerned, it was primo. For two weekends in a row, Werner held a small group of adults captive in a hotel room while he talked, preached, joked, expounded, and got heavy with them. He wouldn't even let them get up to pee until a scheduled break. Amazingly enough, they sat and listened to him. He had been right all along! He did indeed have something to say. At the end of the program, he asked everyone, "Did you get it?" They all responded affirmatively.

Today Wormer Airhead has all the attention he wants. The AST program has brought him both fame and lucre, and a horde of groupies, to whom he is like a living god. Though the AST programs are run by underlings now, Werner still deigns to abuse audiences in large halls. He is at the hub of a humming little empire now, the prince that he always wanted to be.

The AST program costs $700 a pop and still takes two weekends. Seminars are held in most urban areas. For further information, dial 1-777-YUGETIT.

Chapter

5

Media for Personal Growth

In the new age, the medium most definitely is the message. And in the past few years that message has exploded in every direction and in every form—from books and magazines to audio and video cassettes. The following is our selection of the finest media for personal growth. Now you can read, listen, and watch your way to higher consciousness.

The Great Book of the Near-Dead

HAVE YOU HAD a rotten near-death experience? A lot of people have. Thanks to CPR (cardiopulmonary resuscitation), literally thousands of people have dropped dead (mostly due to heart attacks), only to be brought back to life minutes later. Did they have textbook near-death experiences? Did they see the white light? Were they drawn to the light joyfully, calm and serene? No—the odds are excellent that they were terrified, disoriented, and confused. The worst part of the whole thing is when other people ask you what your near-death experience was like, it's humiliating to fess up to the fact that you were so scared, you almost died.

Well, if you've had one near-death experience, you may have another. But next time, wouldn't you like to be dignified, calm, and at one with the universe? *The Great Book of the Near-Dead* is your ticket to a better, more enjoyable death experience next time around.

You'll learn to see the white light, feel at one with the universe, and bound gleefully into the afterlife. Thanks to *The Great Book of the Near Dead,* you can be confident that the next time you die, or almost die, you'll do it easily, correctly, and with style. If you are revived, you'll garner the admiration of those around you as you describe how you casually merged with the cosmos. For a free review copy, dial toll-free 1-777-NEARDED.

Eating Your Way to Enlightenment

Pigging Out on the Path
by Chubs Haggendaz

EATING YOUR WAY TO ENLIGHTENMENT: *Pigging Out on the Path* is about treading the unique Way known as the tantra of food. On the tantric path, desires are neither suppressed nor ignored. They are exploited to their fullest extent, savored without reservation, and witnessed with utter detachment all the while.

Enter Chubs Haggendaz, the corpulent visionary author of *Eating Your Way to Enlightenment.* In this stunning work, he describes a method of eating oneself into "sacred oblivion," the Nirvana of total satiety. This path, he says, "is for those to whom food is like God itself, to whom a piece of cheesecake seems not unlike a sacred mountain."

What about the claims that obesity is unhealthy and that a perfectly fit body is essential to spiritual growth? "Nonsense," dismisses Haggendaz, who says that "fat is beautiful, and more is merrier." The overweight individual, he claims, is perfectly adapted to the Path of Eating. "Some other paths require tough, muscular types. But this one is for people who are expanding in all ways."

Haggendaz does more than theorize about inner and outer growth. He outlines specific techniques for pigging out on the path. Perhaps the most intriguing of these methods is the nighttime fridge raid. Says Haggendaz, "Such a raid must be approached with exquisite care and timing. It is not a casual undertaking. You must lust after the contents of the refrigerator from the very depths of your soul. That level of commitment is truly Pigging Out on the Path."

It is readily apparent that Haggendaz has broken the scales with this book. Consider this highly recommended reading.

The New Best Seller From
CHUBBS HAGGENDAZ
Eating Your Way To
ENLIGTENMENT

A Condo Dweller's Guide to Tipi Living

by Ishi Apartamento

IN THE TRANSITION from the sixties to the eighties, a lot of back-to-the-landers wound up off the farm and in condominiums. Stuck in urban and suburban environments, these condo dwellers have little in their lifestyle to remind them of the days of barefoot-in-the-grass, communal, down-home country living. But this doesn't mean that their dreams are forgotten.

A Condo Dweller's Guide to Tipi Living is an answer to those dreams. Ishi Apartamento presents a way to bring the free-loving, frolicking sixties into your urban dwelling today. The answer, he says, is to erect a tipi in your living room. It's an answer so simple, so easy, it's amazing that

no one has thought of it sooner. Now, whether you live in a thirty-story high-rise or a suburban development, you can live like the Native American that you've always wanted to be.

A Condo Dweller's Guide to Tipi Living explains how to set up your tipi with pillows and cushions, animal skins, and a hibachi in the center for cooking and warmth. Ishi Apartamento also explains how to turn your clothes closet into a smokehouse and how to hunt small animals in local parks. Now you can live the dream of the sixties wherever you dwell!

A Condo Dweller's Guide to Tipi Living is available at fine bookstores everywhere.

Do-It-Yourself
FIREWALKING

So you didn't roast your feet—but you still got burned!

Come on—there's no way in the world it should cost $350 to run across a few hot coals yelling, "cool moss, cool moss." Yet that's exactly what people are paying at firewalks all across the country.

Now, for only $65, you can have your own Do-It-Yourself Firewalking Kit—complete with barbecue, charcoal, lighter fluid, and matches. You supply the positive affirmations, and you're ready to sink your piglets into a searing 1,000-degree pit.

The Do-It-Yourself Firewalking Kit is great for parties and family get-togethers. And you can use it hundreds of times for only a fraction of what it would cost to attend just one high-powered self-improvement seminar.

You'll be the talk of your neighborhood with the Do-It-Yourself Firewalking Kit.

Condo Dweller's Guide to TIPI LIVING

by Ishi Apartamento

The Home Jacuzzi Birth Book

by Sitz Kneipp

In the fifties, we had birth with drugs and forceps. In the sixties, we had Lamaze and Leboyer. In the seventies, we had midwives and birthing chairs. And now, in the eighties, we have the home Jacuzzi birth!

In *The Home Jacuzzi Birth Book*, author Sitz Kneipp describes the step-by-step procedure for delivering your child into a bubbling broth, in the privacy of your own home. The Jacuzzi, he claims, is the ideal environment for a baby to enter when making the escape from the womb. "It is warm, it is in motion, it is effervescent but not too rough, and it makes a pleasing noise. The Jacuzzi was built with childbirth in mind, there is no question about it."

Kneipp, who is outspoken about this method of birthing, claims that a home Jacuzzi birth is easy on the mother and allows for the participation of family and friends. "The bigger the tub, the more people you can put in it. If you've got one of those really large Jacuzzis, you can throw a first-ever birthday party for the new arrival."

On the down side, the author cautions expectant parents to prepare the tub properly. "Put a little iodine in the water, that's all. If your tub contains the usual water-cleaning agents, they can bleach the baby. This is undesirable." Kneipp also cautions to turn the water jet pressure down to low. "If the jets are on too hard, the baby will shoot off like a water polo ball. You do not want that."

All caveats aside, *The Home Jacuzzi Birth Book* is a thorough endorsement of hot tub delivery. Comments Kneipp, "It beats being yanked upside down and whacked on the butt."

The Home Jacuzzi Birth Book is available at bookstores everywhere.

The Home Jacuzzi BIRTH BOOK

by Sitz Kneipp

I'm O.K. but You're Not

by Roberto Manicotti

IN THIS PRACTICAL guide to personal psychology and identity, Roberto Manicotti strikes back at decades of apologists who have claimed that all humans are both equal and valuable. In *I'm O.K. but You're Not,* Manicotti frankly discusses the fact that the world is home to a variety of jerks, creeps, nitwits, finks, dinks, and cretins. An intelligent, productive individual has every right to identify such undesirables and to brush such people briskly out of his or her way.

In *I'm O.K. but You're Not,* Manicotti also fully articulates his controversial "blame therapy," in which you learn to chew people out at their own expense, and walk away satisfied and relieved. "If someone is really a creep," he offers, "then why not immediately communicate that to them? You are simply offering the truth. Otherwise you will be deceptive, pretending that they are acceptable to you."

While detractors of Manicotti's theories assert that "blame therapy" can give rise to gratuitous criticism and harassment of others, Roberto himself is unconvinced. "They're just mumbling fools," he responds coolly.

I'm O.K. but You're Not definitely redefines the concept of tolerance of others and empowers the reader with a sense of combat where there was once simpering acceptance of inferiors. Stimulating reading!

I'M OKAY
BUT YOU'RE NOT

Roberto Manicotti

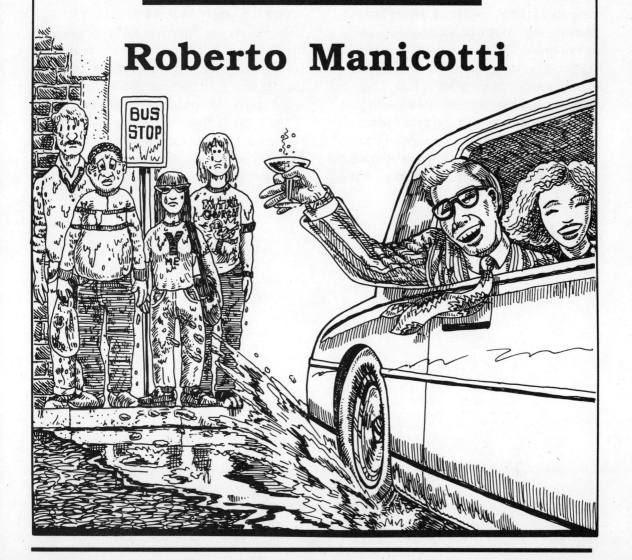

The Cosmic Snafu

by God Knows Who

IF YOU READ any text from a major religion or spiritual philosophy, you will quickly discover the belief that the universe is an intelligent, orderly place to live, in which there exist a variety of inflexible rules.

In his book, God Knows Who explains the random factor in the universe, a factor that operates at all times. The Cosmic Snafu is the unexpected Maybe that doesn't care about gravity, that has no regard for timing and is unconcerned with how a person's day is going. "There really is luck," he explains frankly. "Sometimes it's with you, and sometimes everything gets flushed right down the tubes. If you spend your time trying to figure out what in your karma caused that experience, you're way off the track. The fact is, the Cosmic Snafu sometimes hammers you for no good reason at all. You might win the lottery and then contract some exotic disease that leaves you with two months to live."

In *The Cosmic Snafu,* God Knows Who offers some unsettling possibilities. If you accept his assertion that there is in fact a universal Maybe, then you must reexamine the notion of self-determination. "Sure, sometimes you're driving your own bus," he explains, "but there are other times when you're riding locked in the truck."

The Cosmic Snafu is a well-thought-out challenge to the notion that we each create our own personal reality. "We don't—that's all," says the author.

Money Talks

The Prophet Motive
by Mona Bologna

SOMETIME SEVERAL CENTURIES ago, someone got the notion that the purest spiritual advice is free. According to this line of thought, those who are truly clairvoyant or spiritually gifted should give generously of themselves at no charge.

Bulldooky, says Mona Bologna, author of *Money Talks.* The clairvoyant who fails to charge, she argues, is tomorrow's sage on the street. "Money is the main prophet motive," states Bologna. "Your knowledge and insight are valuable. Part of your job is to charge whatever the market will bear."

In *Money Talks,* Mona debunks the notion of free spiritual guidance and sets the scene for a highly profitable career for modern prophets. "If you were a welder, would you do your work for free? Of course not. You'd charge for every minute of your labor, plus materials, plus travel. The All-Seeing Eye is the toolbox of the psychic or seer. Every time you use it, set the meter and charge, charge, charge." Bologna likens the ability to see the future to manned space flight. "Shooting astronauts into space is extremely costly, and nobody bats an eye at the price. If you can send your consciousness out into deep space, that's worth plenty." Mona Bologna gives practical advice on fee schedules, setting up spreadsheets, and developing a solid financial portfolio. As for how to deal with those who still believe that the best psychic advice is free: "Give them a piece of exquisitely convincing misinformation, and send them out the door."

Money Talks is available at bookstores everywhere.

Steve Heartburn / Musical Boredom

STEVE HEARTBURN IS back with his latest "acoustic sculpture," *Musical Boredom*. With a few easy strokes of his keyboard, Steve Heartburn has given literal meaning to the term "bored to death" in this new album. It's the usual, of course—about ninety solid minutes of soft, lilting electric piano, with plenty of echo and heavy use of the sustain pedal. As in his other thirty acoustic landscapes, Heartburn is out to relieve the world of stress. This he does faithfully well. There is virtually no stress possible while listening to this album. However, neither breathing nor allowing the heart to beat seems necessary either.

Steve Heartburn is a genius for slipping the listener into a somnolent, narcoleptic, catatonic, or comatose state with just a few notes. As with his last album, *New Anesthesia,* Heartburn warns the buyer of his music not to listen while driving. Fatalities have resulted from such practice. Several listeners have sailed through highway guard rails while stupefied by Steve's "quieting sounds." Buyers are advised not to eat while listening, as well. At least three listeners have perished face down in their breakfast cereal, and still another aspirated on his tofu. Truly, Steve Heartburn is killing us softly with his song.

If listening to hours of rainfall is your idea of a wild time, if the sound of a pine tree shaking in the wind stimulates you to a frenzied peak, then you'll love *Musical Boredom* by Steve Heartburn. Don't miss the latest stereophonic soporific from this acclaimed artist! Available wherever records and tapes are sold.

Hand Jobs: Sex, Palmistry, and Your Career

by Gina Lingus

ONE OF THE exciting aspects of the New Age is the way that forward-thinking entrepreneurs are updating old occupations. In *Hand Jobs: Sex, Palmistry, and Your Career,* author Gina Lingus offers a new approach to the profession of palmistry.

"Remember what happened to the escort business," she notes. "For decades, you could barely give escorts away. Then, escort agencies started to offer a broader range of services, and bingo, they started to make serious money. Now that whole industry is booming. Palmistry offers an excellent opportunity to employ sexual talents. You tell a client about their love line, then you start to talk with them about sex. If they seem receptive, offer them something more."

In palmistry, notes Lingus, the client expects privacy, expects to be told intimate secrets, and is looking for something. "Why not jump at the opportunity? Seize the moment. They don't know what you're going to tell them in the first place. But they really want to be stroked. You can lend someone a helping hand in a way that they can really use. I mean, talk about relieving someone's tension."

In *Hand Jobs: Sex, Palmistry, and Your Career,* Gina Lingus has pointed out a new direction for a profession whose ranks have thinned in recent years. "As the number of strip joints decreases," she claims, "you're going to see a lot more 'Reader & Advisor' signs in our cities."

Hand Jobs: Sex, Palmistry, and Your Career is available in most bookstores.

The Whole Brain Tapes

HOW MANY TIMES in your life have you said "I've got half a mind to . . ."? You may not have even realized it at the time, but you were being scientifically correct. Most people walk around through life using just half a mind. They engage either the creative, expansive, curious right side of the brain or the orderly, focused, organized left side. But rarely is there a balance between the two. That is, until now. Now you can enjoy a whole brain, fully active and synchronized, with the Mega-Subliminal Mind Melting Tapes.

How does the term *psychoacoustic* sound to you? Pretty scientific, eh? That's exactly what you can expect from the makers of the Whole Brain Mega-Subliminal Mind Melting Tapes. By listening to these tapes daily, you actually melt the left and right hemispheres of your brain into one solid mass. The result? Complete access to all your brain cells at any moment. This is surely the pinnacle of neuroscience.

How do the tapes work? It's a secret. What are the subliminal messages? They're a secret, too. What does *Mega-Subliminal* mean? That's a patented secret, as well. Don't worry, though. The tapes are advertised in holistic magazines, so you know they're totally aboveboard. If you're ready to embark upon the brain adventure of a lifetime, here's what you can expect from the tapes:

Photographic Memory: You'll remember some photographs that you've seen, especially baby pictures!

Increased Retention: If you have to urinate, you'll be able to wait a few minutes longer than usual before going!

Enhanced Immunity: Whenever you're not sick, your immune system will keep you well!

Creative Visualization: Whenever you take drugs, you'll hallucinate like a madman!

Hyperintelligence: You'll begin to feel just like Einstein!

Never before has humanity been offered so much evolutionary potential for such a low, low price. But you must act fast, because there are only 147,000 of these cassette packages. When they're gone, they're gone! For a beautiful, full-color glossy brochure jam-packed with scientific language, or to place your order, dial toll-free 1-777-MELTING.

The Great Goddess

Organizing Your Pocketbook
by
Clara Wilkins Leadbeater

BY CONTINUING TO carry bags, women participate in an age-old female tradition which has its roots in a cosmic archetype. So says Clara Wilkins Leadbeater, author of *The Great Goddess: Organizing Your Pocketbook.*

Around 3000 B.C., at the time of the Sumerian expansion, women carried large, flexible handwoven baskets, in which they stored a variety of personal effects. These items ranged from pieces of clothing, to jewelry, to the dark, powdered clay that Sumerian women used to color their cheekbones.

Around 1400 B.C., at the beginning of the Shang Dynasty, Chinese women carried ornate bags made of highly durable hemp cloth. The bags could be tied shut with a cord and were used to hold grooming materials, including hairbrushes and face powders.

Around A.D. 475, during the early flourishing of Nigerian civilization, African women toted soft leather bags adorned with tassles and animal teeth. In the bags were kept beads, gold ornaments, and a paste used to adorn various body parts.

Today, women of all nations continue to carry some sort of container for their small belongings—a cloth or leather bag, or even small pieces of luggage. In such a pocketbook, you will find keys, cologne, hairbrushes, gum, a mirror, credit cards, mascara, lipstick, pens, and hundreds of other accoutrements of modern life.

Leadbeater asserts that the pocketbook is in fact an extension of the female soul and that the bag must be well maintained and revered. As Leadbeater puts it, "The urgency of organizing one's pocketbook is at the heart of women's issues today."

Drawing on a wealth of historical knowledge, the author deftly demonstrates that the pocketbook is in fact the single most widely used personal effect in female history. Over the course of 800 long and tedious pages, Leadbeater continues to pound away at her theme about the significance of the pocketbook. The last one-third of this opus is devoted entirely to organizing a pocketbook, with specific instructions for making maximum use of the bag's carrying power. Leadbeater also introduces the revolutionary "icky bag," a separate, zippered plastic bag used for carrying nail polish, perfume, mousse, and other spillable cosmetic items.

The Great Goddess: Organizing Your Pocketbook is a one-of-a-kind, groundbreaking work that sets new standards in the study of women's history and furthers a greater understanding of the human condition. Available at bookstores everywhere.

THE GREAT·GODDESS

ORGANIZING·YOUR·POCKETBOOK

BY CLARA·WILKINS·LEADBEATER

The Lounge Lizard's Guide to New Age Lingo

by Swifty Slade

THE SINGLES SCENE is an ever-changing world of fashions, topics of conversation, and new, creative come-ons. Thanks to the emergence of the New Age, people's values are changing, and so is the way they speak. If you want to make it with someone these days, it isn't enough to wear a Banana Republic safari jacket and blow-dry your hair. You've got to be able to speak the language of a new era of human consciousness.

Author Swifty Slade takes the reader into the labyrinth of fern bars, health clubs, supermarkets, and bookstores, and tells you how to charm the pants off new acquaintances with disarming, humanistic New Age lingo. "The stereotypical lounge lizard is out, except in a few remote social outposts in Texas and the Southwest," explains Slade. "If you want to wind up in bed with someone these days, it isn't enough to pack a condom and make good eye contact. You've got to zing the other person with the appropriate jargon at the right moment."

Swifty Slade offers a set of what he calls "surefire verbal winners." In *The Lounge Lizard's Guide to New Age Lingo,* he updates a variety of smooth lines for establishing rapport:

1. Instead of telling someone that you noticed him or her from across the room, say, "I picked right up on your energy from the other side of the room."

2. Don't compliment your prospective partner on the color of his or her eyes. Instead, make excellent eye contact and say, "Has anyone ever told you that you give off strong positive vibrations? You must have a powerful aura."

3. Ask what astrological sign the person was born under, and be prepared to share yours. No matter what sign the other person is, say how compatible it is with yours. Mention that the person seems very smart, like a Sagittarius.

4. Indicate that you are at least somewhat psychic and that you get a good feeling about the other person that you just can't put into words. Say that you're interested in a deep, meaningful personal relationship.

5. Casually mention that you know how to do Yoga. This is considered exotic and hints of sexual experimentation. Mention the "G Spot." Say that you're a lucid dreamer. Tell the person you'd like to astral-project with him or her.

6. Tell the other person that you believe two people can be drawn together by fate, and ask if he or she believes in karma and reincarnation.

7. Comment on how healthy the other person looks. Suggest that he or she seems to be in very good shape. Hint that you'd like to know for sure. Say that you work out daily.

8. As the other person warms up to you, let on that you are very generous and open-hearted and that you always like to satisfy someone else's needs before your own.

If you have made it successfully through a conversation using all of the above material, says Swifty, you can all but count your chickens. *The Lounge Lizard's Guide to New Age Lingo* is a must for anyone who wants to stay up to date and romantically active in these new, changing times. Available at bookstores everywhere.

Akashic Record: The CD of the Universe

THE AKASHIC RECORD has always been a big deal. Clairvoyants and seers describe it as a record of all that has ever occurred. To find out anything that has ever happened, you need only tune in to the Akashic Record. But what about the other 99.9 percent of humanity, the rest of us louts who just don't have fully developed ESP? Well, thanks to the wonders of modern technology, you don't have to worry your crown chakra anymore, because the Akashic Record has just been released on CD. This is sound like you've never, ever heard before!

The Akashic Record on CD lets you catch up on what you've missed. Ever wonder what Cleopatra and Julius Caesar talked about? Now you can listen in and hear for yourself exactly what went on. While you're getting familiar with this handsome CD, tune in to the original Sermon on the Mount in all its splendor. Or drop in on some ancient Babylonian domestic disputes and hear what couples used to fight about. You'll discover that things really haven't changed.

Now there is no such thing as missing episodes of *Star Trek,* or anything else. If it has happened, it's on CD!

The Akashic Record on CD is available at fine music stores everywhere.

The New Age Book List

WHAT WOULD THE New Age be without books? After all, the printed word is a potent delivery system for New Age thought and ideologies. The following is a list of current New Age titles. Each of these volumes is essential to the well-stocked New Age library.

That Was Zen, This Is Tao, by La Choy

Adventures at the Diamond Sutra Dude Ranch, by Billy the Tulku and the Karma Kid

Hello Dalai, by Burgess Rimpoche

Wicca Dicka Doo, by Alister Crumley

History of the Rastacrucians, by Yellowman Rosencreuz

Fun Signs, by B. Sirius

A Clairvoyant's Guide to Unforeseen Circumstances, by Edgar Crazey

The Aquarium Gospel of Jacques the Cousteau, by Levi and Strauss

The Opening of the Clown Chakra, by Swami Beyondananda

The Egyptian Book of Dead Jokes, by Pharoah Hohotep

Silver Cord Extensions for Long-Distance Astral Travel, by C. W. Bedwetter

Everybody Needs Samadhi Sometime, by Paramahansa Yogananda Parlez-Vous?

Nirvana Nervosa: Dieting to Higher Consciousness, by Oedipus Anorexia

The Midget Psychic Who Escaped from Prison, by a small medium at large

Past Life Savings and Loans, by Rajneesh Baksheesh

Let Us Hold Hands and Contact the Living, by Sybil Sleek

I Never Metaphysics I Didn't Like, by Will Tulku Rogers

Here Today, Sodom Gomorrah, by Billy Graham Crackers

The Book of the Whoopi: Take Two Medicine Wheels and Send Up Smoke Signals in the Morning, by Born Bear

Silver Dollar Mind Control, by Hi Ho Silva

The Bigfat Gita, by Charles Chubchakra

The Secrets of Flounderhorn, by Peter and Eileen Caddyshack

Tibetan Break-Dancing, by Hopalong Rampa

The Complete Guide to Debirthing, by Leonard Bore

A Knife Thrower's Guide to Acupuncture, by Guy Fat Fang

The Incarnation of Hip: How Hip Happened, by Maynard G. Kerouac

There's No Mind, Never Mind—and Zen Some, by Roshi Alzheimer

I Think Therefore I Ching, by La Choy

Genesis and the Old Testicle, or Great Balls of Fire and the Big Bang, by Salt Peter

Don't Fall Off a Limb, by Surely Deranged

Laya Yoga: Sex and the Single Swami, by Swami Orchid

Chew the Root, Gnaw the Bark: A Guide to Raw Foods, by Victoras Mungbean

Soy Vey: Jewish Vegetarian Cookery, by Menachem Tempeh

Chapter

6

Go to Health

Now, thanks to the emergence of holistic health, you can look and feel tremendous every day, for the rest of your life! The following holistic health resources are designed to help you make the most of living in a mortal body. Choose your favorites from this smorgasbord of healthy possibilities as you consciously evolve to a higher state of well-being.

Macroneurotics

IN THE EARLY 1930s a young Irishman named George O'Sowhat headed for Japan, where he recovered from an almost terminal case of severely inflamed hemorrhoids. Attributing his Lourdes-like recovery to his diet of seaweed, brown rice, and shaved fish, he started Macroneurotics.

According to O'Sowhat, all of human history revolves around diet. The United States, he predicted, will succumb to the final mortal blow of the hamburger and an inadequate intake of brown rice. The space program will self-destruct because man was not designed to eat mush from a tube.

The Macroneurotic diet is designed with nature in mind. According to O'Sowhat, "If natural creatures will eat a morsel, then that same morsel is suitable for humans." Hence the Macroneurotic credo: "Fifty thousand flies can't be wrong." If you leave a five-pound plate of shaved fish, seaweed, and brown rice out in the hot sun, it will draw 50,000 flies. This is proof enough to followers of Macroneurotics that the same fare is ideal for humans.

The dietary guru also had his own unique ideas about beauty. "To be truly attractive," he wrote, "you must be gaunt enough that your head looks like a hollowed skull with parchment spread over it, and your hips must be as thin as an Oriental fan." There is no question that O'Sowhat redefined beauty, setting a new, revolutionary standard for his followers.

The single most important aspect to becoming a true Macroneurotic is that you must become thoroughly obsessive about food. It is not enough to eat seaweed, rice, and shaved fish. If it rains outside, you must ask, "What should I eat to balance the effect of the rain?" If, on the other hand, you receive some bad news, you should ask, "What have I eaten to deserve such misfortune?" You must also eat everything, including soup, with chopsticks.

Macroneurotics wholeheartedly embraces the Oriental theory of yin and yang. Heavy foods such as meats and cheeses are very yang, while lighter, sweeter foods are yin. The idea is to balance the two, for perfect harmony. If you wish to eat a hot fudge sundae, for example, then you should add to it a couple of scoops of raw ham. Cheese fondue, on the other hand, should be eaten with ripe bananas. By adjusting your dietary intake in this manner, claims O'Sowhat, "You will become enlightened, and Zen some."

For more information on Macroneurotics, read *Rice Is Nice* by Hoochy Kuchi, or *Fifty Thousand Flies Can't Be Wrong* by George O'Sowhat.

Acupuncher

AMONG THE CHINESE systems of health care, no set of methods is more powerful than acupuncher. In acupuncher, a variety of points and zones of the body are stimulated manually to produce specific healing results. The acupunchurist uses his or her fist to strike, pound, pummel, or otherwise energize the particular therapeutic points for whatever ailment is being treated.

Dr. Sugar Ray Chang, one of the foremost acupuncherists alive today, describes some practical applications of this unique health science. "A lot of people have trouble sleeping these days. I use a blinding fast roundhouse to the temple to put them out. Acupuncher is very effective. It's especially good for anesthesia." And so it seems. Acupuncherists claim great success with mental and emotional disorders as well.

"Let's say that a person is mean and argumentative," poses Dr. Chang. "A quick flurry of left and right hooks to all parts of the torso and face usually remedies this condition, creating in its place a more subdued, humble mood. On the other hand, if someone is lethargic, a sharp slap to either cheek will stimulate them and make them more alert."

Regular clients claim that acupuncher has made a dramatic difference for them. "My body is totally unlike when I started," comments one individual. "After about the fifth session, I had a lot more color in my face, and it felt like every muscle in my body was tender from the healing process."

If you'd like further information on acupuncher, write to Dr. Sugar Ray Chang's Acupuncher Center and Boxing Gym, 66 Crackerjack Blvd., New York, NY 10000.

Quang Long Dong Herbal Products

THE CHINESE HAVE enjoyed the benefits of a highly sophisticated system of herbal healing for well over five thousand years. The formulas of the ancient Chinese herbal masters are among the most respected and treasured natural medicines in the world. Until now, however, these formulas have been virtually unavailable to the Western world.

Quang Long Dong is a respected name in Chinese herbal pharmacology. Their new location in New York City makes it possible for the Occidental world to enjoy the cream of herbal formulas. Quang Long Dong's slogan is "Good for your Yin/Yang." Living up to this slogan, they offer a full selection of restorative and rejuvenating products. The following formula descriptions are from the Quang Long Dong catalog.

Long Dong Wow: This formula for men is reputed to "extend vitality." It contains ground goat gonad, wild ram horn, four kinds of ginseng, and fugu-dehydrated puffer fish flesh.

Pee Man Cok: A superb diuretic, Pee Man Cok is the perfect formula for reducing body water. This special medicine stimulates and tonifies the kidneys and bladder. Contains concentrated celery seed extract, asparagus powder, and burro bladder.

Weez Lung Doo: Bronchial congestion and difficult breathing can result in fatigue and poor sleep. This formula opens the breathing passageways and dissolves mucus blockages in the alveoli of the lungs. Contains nail parings, oak bark, and orange rind.

Toe Jamm Goo: When you keep your shoes and socks on for weeks at a time, or walk barefoot in a disease-ridden place, athlete's foot and other podiatric infections can result. Toe Jamm Goo is a topical cream made from mashed goldenseal root, wild yams, and flying fish roe. Smeared generously upon infected feet, it will keep anything else from touching them.

Quong Long Dong Herbal Formulas are made from the finest ingredients available. Each formula comes with a 100 percent satisfaction guarantee. If you don't like something you buy, for any reason, Quong Long Dong will refund your money if you personally hand-deliver the product to their offices during normal business hours. For a catalog of products and prices, write to Quong Long Dong Herbal Products, 56B Houdon St., New York, NY 01002. Or call toll free 1-777-YINYANG.

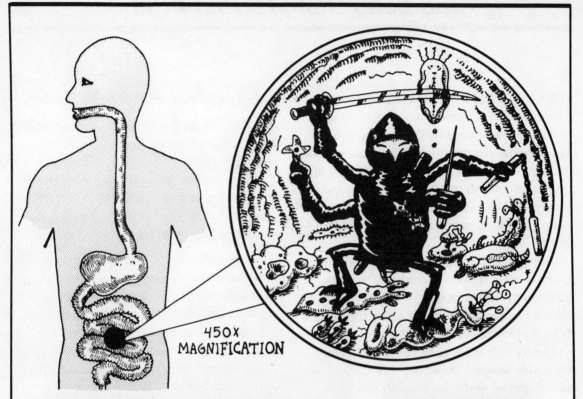

450x
MAGNIFICATION

INTESTINAL NINJA

◄ In order to stay healthy, you need healthy intestinal bacteria. The problem is, though, that the "friendly" bacteria in the human GI tract may in fact be too friendly. Evidence suggests that it is all too easy for our friendly intestinal bacteria to be overcome by more powerful microorganisms. The result is indigestion and disease.

◄ The folks at Zampow Labs have bred a new strain of healthy bacteria designed to fight invaders to the death inside your intestines. Intestinal Ninja is the pure, undiluted strain of *Acidophilus violentus* bacteria. This bacteria doesn't roll over, lay down, and die like most intestinal bacteria. *Acidophilus violentus* hides out in the folds of the colon. When unfriendly bacteria come along, the Intestinal Ninja ambush the intruders, decimate them, and ship them off through the bowels.

◄ Why suffer from weak digestion when you can have galvanized intestines instead? Intestinal Ninja knocks the crap out of unfriendly bacterial intruders and lives to fight another day!

◄ Intestinal Ninja is available at health food stores everywhere.

End Animal Testing

THERE SEEMS TO be no end to this crime. Every day, thousands of animals undergo unusual and unnecessary tests. The companies who subject helpless creatures to these extreme procedures have no conscience whatsoever and need to be stopped. At least, so says BLEAT, or the Big League to End Animal Testing.

According to BLEAT spokesman Nelson Burroff, animal testing is rampant. "We've seen cows forced to take the SATs, we've seen rats cramming for their law boards, and we've witnessed cats taking high-level French comprehension exams." Burroff says that BLEAT's objective is to eliminate all such testing in both industry and government. "It's okay to be a dumb bunny," he insists. "What possible benefit can the IRS gain by making gerbils study calculus? It just doesn't make any sense. And that's why we're out to end testing."

At the same time that BLEAT is creating greater awareness of this issue, supporters of animal testing point to its benefits. NASA Director Ward Bingo sums up the testing of chimpanzees for space flight in one terse line. "If we hadn't tested the chimps first, men would have gone up into space and been blown to pieces."

"That's true," acknowledges Burroff. "But on the other hand, it is senseless and cruel to administer Russian Literature exams to nubian goats. Where do you draw the line?"

Apparently, BLEAT draws the line very clearly, seeking a total ban on animal testing. Burroff pleads, "Let's let dogs fetch sticks instead of undergoing Wechsler I.Q. tests."

For information on animal testing, write to BLEAT, 2221 Housatonic Dr., Cambridge, MA 02139.

Ha Ha Yoga for the Millions

ONE OF THE keys to health is a strong, flexible body. For thousands of years, sages in the Far East have practiced Yoga to achieve a high level of health and peace of mind. Pundit Rupeeananda has translated the ancient Yoga scriptures into today's language and has brought the techniques of Ha Ha Yoga to the West. "A flexible body breeds a flexible mind," states Rupeeananda, who operates the Ha Ha Yoga Fitness Center in Chicago.

At the heart of Ha Ha Yoga is a series of 108 contortions designed to stretch to the limits every fiber of muscle, cartilage, and tendon in your entire body. "Twisting your body is just a metaphor for the twists that occur in your life. You must learn to radiate light and love, no matter what your position may be," preaches Rupeeananda, who charges over $100 an hour for private lessons.

Students flock to the Ha Ha Yoga Center to learn the deepest secrets of this exotic Yogic science. Wagner Bent, a five-year student of Rupeeananda's, describes his experience with this system. "Now I can scratch the middle of my back with my tongue. I mean, is that a sign of health, or what?" In fact, the interest in this Yoga is so great that Pundit Rupeeananda has written an extensive manual, *Ha Ha Yoga for the Millions.* In it he describes the techniques

that have garnered him fame and fortune. The following three methods are among the 108 Ha Ha Yoga techniques:

Heel-to-Ear Pose: Wrap your left leg around the back of your head, and block your right ear with your left heel, while standing on your right leg, with your arms stretched toward the sky. In this position, breathe deeply for five full minutes, while concentrating on your third eye. With diligent practice, your hearing will become deafeningly acute.

Nose Walk: Lying face down with your arms behind your back, press your nose against the ground and use it to drag you, inch by inch, for approximately ten feet. This will strengthen your sense of smell and will enable you to sniff out dinner from a distance of two miles.

Practice this every morning for forty days.

Butt Spin: Sitting on your butt with your legs extended above the ground, use your hands to spin you around quickly in a clockwise circle, fifty times fast. If practiced for a full year, this will slim and toughen your buttocks and will enhance digestion.

It is readily apparent that Pundit Rupeeananda is a unique man with a great vision. Through the secrets of Ha Ha Yoga, he is helping mere mortals to unravel the mysteries of the body and to develop extraordinary health. For more information on Ha Ha Yoga, or to order a copy of *Ha Ha Yoga for the Millions,* write to the Ha Ha Yoga Center, 1010 East Asana Drive, Chicago, IL 34721.

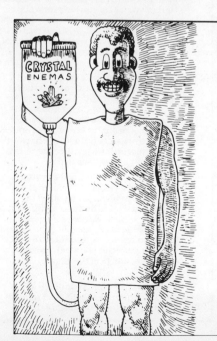

The Horror of Carob

IT'S HARD TO know how this whole scam got started. Carob, also known as locust bean, is a large red pod that grows on an evergreen tree in warm climates. It is believed to be the "locust" eaten by John the Baptist in the wilderness, and it is used as a stabilizer in food products, in papermaking, and in curing tobacco. So far so good. But probably, somewhere around the 1960s, some completely deranged health food freak ordained carob as a substitute for chocolate, and the world of confections has not been safe since.

Even the name "locust bean" should give you some sort of hint just how bad this stuff really is. It tastes how you might imagine ground bugs would. Nonetheless, thousands of pounds of this horror go into "healthy" cookies, candy bars, cakes, ice cream, and flavored drinks.

Carob is to chocolate what a cheap vinyl purse is to prime rib. The similarities are truly imaginary. On top of that, carob tastes just plain bad on its own. However, it is now apparent that carob is a potent hallucinogen which works on some, but not all, of the people who eat it. This drug acts in an insidious manner, erasing any gustatory or olfactory memory, causing otherwise sane consumers to remark, "Gee, this really does taste just like chocolate."

Why eat something that tastes like it came from a dust pan? Ask for chocolate.

YUCATÁN GO JUICE

Aromatherapy

Take a Whiff for Health

FRAGRANT ESSENTIAL OILS have been used in cosmetics and perfumery for ages and are respected for a wide variety of pharmaceutical purposes. Now these essences are being recognized as powerful olfactory healers. The science of Aromatherapy is about breathing your way to a more energetic, vital self by inhaling specific fragrances. "The nostrils are the closest holes to your brain," explains Jean Pierre Nazale of the Aromatherapy Center in Paris. "Fragrances go right to your brain cells, and they supersaturate the entire thinking organ, with exquisitely healthful consequences."

According to Nazale, scents are the remedies of a new, more enlightened culture. "Think about it," he says. "Would you rather take an aspirin, which might eat a hole through your stomach, or take a good headful of rose petals?" The argument is convincing.

Citing the nose as the major pleasure organ of the face, Nazale quips "Incense is good sense."

Practitioners of Aromatherapy are certainly making money up the nose, peddling fragrant elixirs for every possible health complaint. Another group of elixirs is available for those who want a radiant spirit, a clear mind, an open heart, and an empty wallet.

If you'd like to sniff out the possibilities of Aromatherapy in your own life, write to the Aromatherapy Center, 347 Rue Nez, Paris, France.

The Pond Scum Diet

HUMANITY TODAY IS afflicted by a great assortment of maladies, from heart disease to cancer, AIDS, emphysema, colitis, diabetes, and so on. Each of these diseases represents a breakdown in the functional harmony of the body/mind apparatus. At the root of most if not all of these disorders is improper nutrition. Yet it seems impossible to load the body with all the nutrients needed to maintain glowing health.

It used to be impossible. Now there is Super Blue Pond Scum from Klamath Falls, Oregon. Super Blue Pond Scum is the number-one most concentrated superfood in the world, maybe in the whole universe. It's so simple, it's brilliant.

Here's the theory behind eating concentrated pond scum. The entire animal kingdom originated from a primordial protozoan slime billions of years ago. Since that time, myriads of creatures have evolved, resulting in a complex chain of millions of high-order species. But there is a fundamental biology and ecology to our design. Each of us still has a powerful relationship with the original slime from whence we came. Super Blue Pond Scum is

that slime, in all its gooey, fishy splendor.

Trapped at the bottom of Upper Klamath Lake, Super Blue Pond Scum lies like thick silt, about 85 feet deep. The scum has collected for several hundreds of thousands of years and has become the single most concentrated cache of nutrients known. There is nutrition enough in the silt at the bottom of Klamath Lake to make all of humanity zing with life force. Super Blue Pond Scum is now available bottled, tableted, and packaged in convenient Super Blue Pond Scum Granola Bars. The diet consists of simply substituting Super Blue Pond Scum for all other food, for eighteen months.

The Pond Scum Diet will heal any disease, no matter how severe. Several people have even reportedly arisen from the dead after having Super Blue Pond Scum smeared on their cold, cadaverous foreheads. The Scum is a potent rejuvenator. If you suffer any affliction at all, from constipation to depression, from headaches to hysteria, the Pond Scum Diet will bring you back to full, glowing health. For further information on this panacea, call toll-free 1-777-PNDSCUM.

The Mozart Flower Remedies

FLOWER REMEDIES HOLD a unique place in natural pharmacy. For unlike most other remedies and medicines, flower remedies work on attitude and states of mind as well as upon physical ailments. The Mozart Flower Remedies are the most highly revered of all flower remedies and are known for their dramatic healing properties. Discovered by Dr. Renaldo Mozart of Salzburg, the Mozart Flower Remedies are made by distilling flower petals of various kinds in large vats of fresh stout.

According to Dr. Mozart, a couple of quarts of the remedies daily will improve attitude, stimulate social behavior, and create a feeling of mild invincibility. The following are a few of the remedies and their benefits.

Magic Flute Elixir: For that drooping feeling, this elixir will perk you up, firm you, and give thrust to your activities.

Eine Kleine Nachtformula: The original Mozart sleep aid, this remedy lulls you to sleep with the sounds of music in your head.

Essence of Harpsichordium: For frayed nerves that have been stretched to the limit by life's pressures, this tincture restores harmony to your soul. (Also recommended for keyboard instrumentalists as an aid to improving finger technique.)

Users of the Mozart Flower Remedies report impressive results. Thor Yeoman of Norway writes, "I was just a big burly fellow with no purpose in life. Then I tried the Dr. Mozart Flower Remedies. Now I am a confirmed lunatic and run naked through the streets at night chasing young girls and brandishing a half-eaten leg of lamb. Thank you, Dr. Mozart."

You, too, can change your own life with the Mozart Flower Remedies. For further information, write Dr. Mozart Flower Remedies, 4325 Bauhaus, Salzburg, Austria.

Chapter

7

Food for Thought

Got a healthy body? Great! But what about your mind? You no longer have to settle for just one or the other. Now you can have your holistic body and still enjoy a happy, satisfied mind. The following is a selection of fine programs designed to create exactly the kind of mental makeup you desire for a vigorous, dynamic life.

The John Silly Program

VIRTUALLY EVERYONE IN the New Age knows about John Silly. He invented the sensory-deprivation "floatation" tank, was among the very first researchers to communicate with dolphins, and has explored the uses of LSD more than just about any credible scientist alive today. Don't you wish that you could enjoy the same insights, unusual experiences, and cutting-edge phenomena that John Silly has enjoyed?

Now you can, with the John Silly Program. This is real, live hands-on excitement at its finest, with you at the very center of the cyclone!

In the John Silly Program, you and a dolphin take LSD together in a floatation tank while listening to hours of New Age music and Tibetan gongs. Imagine the thrill, the unbridled intensity, of tripping with Flipper in a small dark tub, completely sealed off from the rest of the world.

And the price? Only $1,150.00 for the most incredible ten hours of your life. From the time you start to get off till the moment you come back down, you'll be in an ecstasy available to a fortunate few.

The John Silly Program is not for everyone. It is for those whose minds are keen, whose hearts are strong, and whose personal commitment to growth extends way past the social norm.

Turn on, tune in, and call today toll-free at 1-777-LSDFISH.

The Altered States Seminar

IF YOU THINK about it, you actually transition from one state of mind to another all day long. One moment you may be elated, the next moment contemplative, then sad, then happy, and so on. Still, all these mental states or moods fall within certain predictable internal parameters. Even smoking marijuana becomes ordinary if practiced frequently.

The Altered States Seminar offers an extraordinary opportunity to step way, way out of your ordinary daily reality, for a few hours or for several months at a time. In the Altered States Seminar, you can start out in a church in Boston and wind up dressed as a cabbage on *Let's Make a Deal*. You'll experience sights, sounds, smells, and sensations completely outside your daily routine.

The Altered States Seminar was created by a group of parapsychologists in response to a growing boredom in our culture. In prehistoric times, man was exposed to fun, excitement, tedium, and life-threatening peril, all in one day. This kept life exciting and offered a variety of opportunities for altered states. Today, however, most people live in an insular, finely structured world that is only too comfortable. Thus the need for the Altered States Seminar.

The seminar works on the basis of surprise. Once you sign up, anything can happen. On your way to the seminar, you may be abducted by terrorists or kidnapped by sinister mobsters and sold on the overseas sex market. One thing is for sure: your experience will alter your state of mind radically, or you get double your money back. Just imagine the fun and excitement of talking your way out of a smuggler's lair in Bangkok, or out of a ward for the criminally insane in a Soviet Gulag. Thrill to the sound of Hell's Angels wheeling around you in an ever tightening circle, and ponder life anew as you are tossed out into a blinding Nepalese snowstorm, buck naked.

If routine has reduced your life to a predictable, static hell, the Altered States Seminar can open up new vistas of mind. Break out of your little world and experience something radically different! For further information, call toll-free 1-777-SURPRIZ.

Electrical Gestalt Therapy

IN CONVENTIONAL GESTALT Therapy, the clients sit in chairs and address "issues" that they have with an imaginary person in an empty chair directly across from them. For example, if you have unresolved problems with your parents, you imagine them sitting across from you, and you address them in whatever ways are necessary to resolve your inner conflicts.

Truth be known, however, there are just some instances in which problems can't be resolved. There are people in one's life with whom there will always be bad, unfinished business. Electrical Gestalt Therapy (EGT) is for those instances. Developed by psychologist Dr. Fritz Blitz, Electrical

Gestalt Therapy is several steps beyond its traditional counterpart.

In EGT, the other chair is in fact an electric chair, completely wired and grounded for a stunning 50,000-watt moon ride for the person who sits in it. And, in contrast to traditional Gestalt Therapy, the individual with whom you have unresolved conflict is really in the chair.

During the therapy session, every attempt is made to end whatever disagreement, dispute, pain, or emotional rift has existed between you, the client, and the other person in question. But there may come a point when it is apparent that no further progress will be made. It is at this

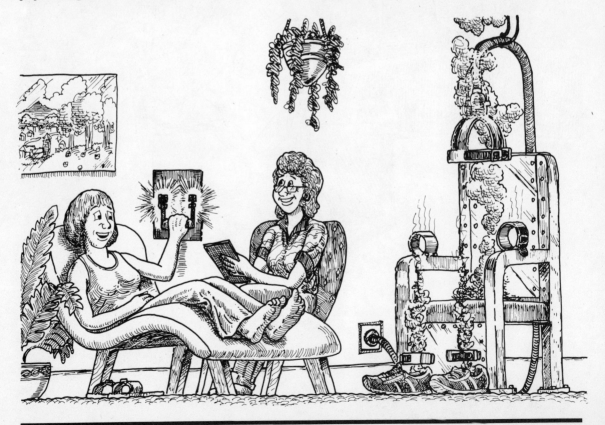

point that Electrical Gestalt Therapy comes into play. With the source of your emotional unease firmly fastened in the chair, you deliver a final monologue, a "closure speech." This gives you ample opportunity to verbalize anything that may otherwise have been left unsaid. With this done, you then flip on the current to the chair and watch your problems go up in smoke.

Dr. Blitz sums it up this way: "This therapy may seem a little radical, and it is. But you would be amazed at just how effective it is for getting rid of the client's unresolved feelings. It is the perfect therapy for the Me Generation."

For information on Electrical Gestalt Therapy, call toll-free 1-777-GESTALT.

Manifesting Reality into Dreams

HOW IS YOUR life going? Really, how are you doing? Have you achieved your heart's desire? Are you where you want to be? Are you actually completely fulfilled?

The honest answers to the above questions are almost always negative. In fact, most people don't ever get what they want, and die unfulfilled. At least, so says Clara Pelfwind, who leads a new workshop, Manifesting Reality into Dreams. "We call it a workshop because it works," states Pelfwind frankly. The premise of Manifesting Reality into Dreams is that you can find self-fulfillment by learning to dream about the things you haven't achieved in life but have always wanted.

Let's say that you wish to be rich and successful. According to Pelfwind, you just have to dream it up. "People who have taken the workshop wind up sleeping more," states Clara, "and they get what they want in their dreams. If you want to, you can be a prince in a dream. Try doing that while you're awake. It'll never happen."

Using a combination of group encounter, sacred dancing, chanting, and designer drugs, Clara Pelfwind teaches workshop participants to dream about whatever they want, in Technicolor, with astounding special effects. Reports one graduate, "My life is the usual boring, dehumanizing stuff. But when I slip between the covers and go to sleep, I'm surfing 45-foot waves and parachuting into the jungle. I'm doing what I've always wanted to, right now."

The unanimous sentiment among graduates is that Manifesting Reality into Dreams offers an opportunity for significant life satisfaction. To learn more about how to maximize your dream time, call toll-free 1-777-DREAMIN.

Abundance Therapy

Overcoming the Blues with Wealth

THERE IS NOW conclusive proof that individuals who are wealthy and comfortable are actually more satisfied with their lives than those who are poor or struggling to get by. A ten-year $32 million survey conducted by the General Accounting Office determined that wealthy individuals—who make up approximately 7 percent of the total population of this country—are in fact a full 68 percent happier overall than those who live at a subsistence level. Of course, many people have suspected this to be the case for a long time. Now we know for sure.

"This bold new finding leads to exciting possibilities in the field of psychotherapy and points the way to new treatments for depression, unhappiness, and general life distress." So says Manfred Hearsay, who conducts an intensive two-week workshop, Abundance Therapy: Overcoming the Blues with Wealth. "To be perfectly frank, once people become rich, a lot of their problems cease." Hearsay's argument is convincing. He explains that in his workshop he teaches participants to devote their full attention to becoming wealthy, to rid themselves of the blues.

"A lot of people think that if they had a little bit more money and one more day off a week, they would be happy," comments Manfred, who is a multimillionaire. "It isn't so. They really need a pile of money, real estate, the works—and unlimited leisure time. Think about it: most folks are concerned about having enough and are unhappy about having to work at all. Being really rich eliminates all those concerns." Drawing from the financial success stories of the Rockefellers, the Vanderbilts, the Kennedys, William Randolph Hearst, and the Mellon family, Hearsay points the way to a future that is brighter, easier, and less troubled. "This isn't to say that you won't have troubles. You'll wonder whether to wear an angora sweater or a silk shirt. These are problems you can deal with."

Successful graduates of the Abundance Therapy intensive workshop agree. Nine of eleven participants who actually have become rich since the workshop claim to be significantly happier and more fulfilled. The cost of the workshop, $12,000, is steep. "But it's worth it," says Hearsay, who claims he doesn't really need the money. If you'd like to learn about the benefits of being rich and how to get that way, call the Abundance Therapy Center toll-free at 1-777-WEALTHY.

Managing Entity Intrusion

PROBABLY ONE OF the most embarrassing, frustrating, and sometimes dangerous things that can happen these days is when the entity that you channel decides to come on through—completely uninvited. In fact, this happens to hundreds of helpless people every day. You're on a date, you lean forward to kiss for the very first time, and POW!—your entity decides that this is the perfect opportunity to launch off into a two-hour monologue on the development of ice sculpture in early Atlantis.

Or worse, you're driving along the freeway at rush hour, heading for an exit ramp in bumper-to-bumper traffic, when your entity comes busting through with good news about the imminent return of the Avatar.

Unwanted entity intrusion is a big problem, especially nowadays, when more and more discarnate souls are eager to talk about life, reality, or whatever else pops into their headless minds. It used to be that entities would wait to be called, but those days are gone. Now they just stroll on into a person's body, take over, and start to chat about any damn thing.

If you're tired of pesky drop-in entities who treat your body like their own, then Managing Entity Intrusion is for you. For further information, dial toll-free 1-777-INTRUDE.

Designer Drugs

Wild Times on the Royal Road

THE PATH TO higher consciousness is the Royal Road, the most spectacular of all journeys. The scenery of the mind is beyond compare, beyond description. Throughout all of human history, people have employed drugs to assist in their explorations. These drugs have varied widely, from the hashish of the Middle East to the balché of the Mayans, the peyote of the Native Americans, and the mushrooms of dozens of cultures. By consuming these drugs, individuals open up what Aldous Huxley called "the doors of perception."

Today, pharmaceutical genius has pioneered an even more advanced group of designer drugs, specifically geared to touring the Royal Road. These drugs are new, exciting, and on the cutting edge of mind exploration technology.

"Nothing comes between me and my designer drugs," says Baby Medicine Shields, director of the Center for Designer Drug Technology. "Whatever it is that your mind desires, we can whip it up in our labs."

The three most popular formulas created in the labs have taken the human mind farther than the shamans of long ago ever dreamed possible:

M&M 28: This exotic psychedelic enables the user to hallucinate at will and to create entire holographic movies inside the mind. The "trip" lasts about thirteen hours, with no apparent side effects, except that it makes perspiration smell like patchouli oil.

Bono: More than any pharmaceutical substance known, Bono induces a state of wild euphoria. Users of the drug must be supervised while under its influence. A little less than 100 micrograms of Bono makes people want to dress in Spandex, grow their hair, grab an electric guitar by the teeth, and scream and wail under hot spotlights. Bono is the definitive cure for performance anxiety.

Pookie Pookie: This drug, which is also called Cute 1, gives the user a supreme case of the warm fuzzies. "It's the Teddy Bear of mind-altering substances," explains Shields. "It makes you feel cute, adorable, warm, lovable, and completely content." Pookie Pookie was originally designed as a chemical-war drug, capable of disarming armies. Today it is taken by thousands of individuals who simply want to feel good about anything and everything.

If you would like to experience tomorrow's mind technology today, write to the Center for Designer Drug Technology, 967 Salamander Drive, Orem, Utah.

Chapter

8

Buyer Be Aware

Throughout human history people have gathered in the marketplace. Even in the New Age it is becoming increasingly obvious that some people were born to chant mantras while others were born to shop. Indeed, as we approach the millenium, we see that the marketplace has again come to occupy a sacred, central place in our society.

To contribute to your shopping experience in the Cosmic Age, we present the following goods as some of the finest accoutrements to a modern lifestyle.

Dowdy 100% Cotton Clothing

JUST HOW NATURAL are you? Do you eat whole grains but wear nylon panty hose? Do you exercise regularly but wear polyester pullovers? If you're going to be all natural, then get yourself into some Dowdy 100% Cotton Clothing.

Dowdy 100% Cotton Clothing is made in Santa Cruz by a devoted group of organic tailors who live in a large commune overlooking the Santa Cruz mountains. The scene couldn't be more natural—and neither could the clothing they produce. The shirts, pants, skirts, dresses, and shorts made by Dowdy 100% Cotton Clothing are strong, durable, washable, and require no ironing. They stay wrinkled all the time, retaining their totally natural look. And all pieces are available in blue, maroon, or natural white. All colored garments are dyed with pure vegetable coloring that is fixed into the material by the sun.

When you wear Dowdy 100% Cotton Clothing you stand out in a crowd. Walking into your office with a new pair of maroon drawstring cotton pants with the patented gusseted crotch, you'll get looks from everyone. In a meeting, you'll be conspicuous in a blue pullover with a lace-up neck. There's no question, everybody around you will know there's nothing synthetic about you. You're all natural.

Standing for all-natural principles is a way of saying, "Hey, I'm tuned in to the natural order of things. I'm seriously organic." What a great way to demonstrate your natural commitment—with Dowdy 100% Cotton Clothing. The loose, easy look will suit your loose, easy disposition. In Dowdy 100% Cotton Clothing, you'll always look ready to pull out a guitar, sit down by the woodstove, and get a good buzz on.

For information on Dowdy 100% Cotton Clothing, dial toll-free 1-777-THECRUZ.

Sacred Feces

HOW MANY TIMES have you heard the expression "holy shit" in your life? You've probably heard it thousands of times. But did you ever ask yourself how that expression ever got started? Sacred Feces is actually something that has been around since the early Egyptian empire. What is it? It's the dehydrated, pressed dung of saints, sages, and masters of the Wisdom. This highly coveted doo-doo is loaded with psychic energy. One small brick of Sacred Feces will empower your entire household with dynamic, sacred vibrations.

The people at Odorono Products in Cincinnati have obtained several hundred kilos of guaranteed first-quality holy shit, which is available in convenient, plastic-sealed four-ounce squares. This divine ordure will supersaturate any living space with pure God vibrations for several years. This first-class caca is the perfect addition to a home altar, meditation room, or Yoga studio.

Each packet of Sacred Feces comes with a signed affidavit guaranteeing authenticity of origin. This product is truly holy shit. To place an order, call toll-free 1-777-POOPOOS.

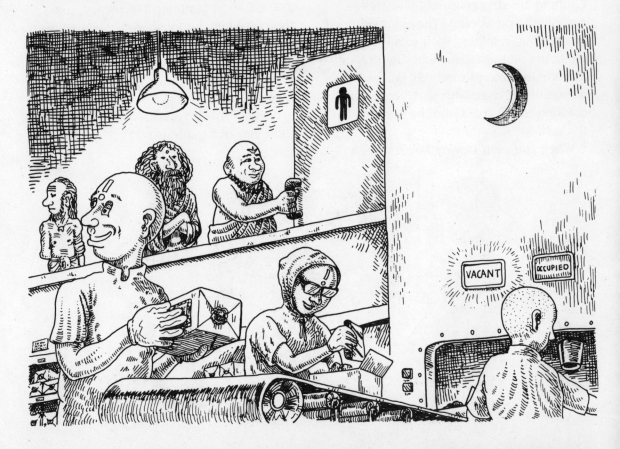

Crystal-Clear Consciousness!

CERTAINLY THE MOST spectacular products to burst upon the New Age scene are crystals. They are absolutely everywhere—on necklaces and earrings, on mantlepieces and altars, as hood ornaments and headbands. Crystals have definitely replaced lava lamps as the number-one category of products of modern times. What is the secret of the success of crystals? How can one explain such a phenomenon, which has seemingly sprung out of nowhere?

The answer to these questions lies in the very nature of crystals themselves. Crystals are beautiful to look at. Quartz crystals and other naturally occurring faceted gemstones conduct light in brilliant and sometimes spectacular ways, creating rainbow effects. Some crystals—such as quartz, Rochelle salt, silicon, germanium, galena, and silicon carbide—also have unique electrical properties and are thus highly prized for the manufacture of electronic equipment.

But even these answers skirt the real issue. For crystals are actually condensed energy, powerfully compact, multifaceted vessels of pure light and intelligence. Crystals, quite simply, are the very essence and memory of the planet Earth itself. They are like a library of fabulous books, each one bearing knowledge about this awesome planet of ours.

At least, this is what aficionados of crystals would lead us to believe. But why are crystals so popular now? Actually, crystals have been popular for thousands of years. Seers, clairvoyants, and necromancers have used crystal balls since time immemorial to divine both the past and the future. The crystal ball is an easily recognizable fixture in any occult novel or movie. The psychic, hunched over the ball, stares deeply into its center and sees what others cannot.

The editorial staff of *In Search of the New Age* spent several months interviewing the top experts on crystals, to determine the truth about these mysterious stones. We have compiled the information according to recommended usage. We believe that you will find the following material inspiring and revealing.

Space Stone: No true New Age voyager would set foot out of doors without the space stone. This crystal is for use during abductions by extraterrestrials. It enables the user to communicate more easily with E.T.'s and to enhance the few precious moments of such extraordinary encounters.

The Record Keeper: Ever wonder where all the lost 78s and 45s went? They are locked up in the cosmic ethers, accessible only through record keepers. Record keepers are large, heavy quartz clusters. To use record keepers, grasp two of them and press them firmly against your ears. You will hear original tunes as you have never heard them before. At first you may not make out all the songs, but with continuous practice, you will hear Cab Calloway, Nelson Eddie, Rudy Vallee, Bill Haley, and Fats Domino, as clear as the day they were recorded.

Meditatos: If you think about it, meditation takes a tremendous amount of time and energy. Meditatos are large geodes that meditate for you. Once you own such a stone, it knows who it belongs to. A meditato stone meditates all day long, absorbing good karma for your use. This leaves you free to pursue other activities.

Mediteenies: These are little meditato stones that you can carry in your pocket or on trips. They purify your energy during business hours or in meetings, and are excellent to carry on a first date.

The Wisdom Eye Crystal: These egg-sized faceted stones are worn directly in the center of the forehead. They can be either woven into headbands or taped directly to the skin between the eyebrows. By

pounding on the stone with the fist or a small mallet, the energy of the stone is released, and the wearer will see stars and visions.

Eat Stones: These dark, heavily veined crystals are designed to help you decide what foods to eat. Bring an Eat Stone with you to the supermarket, and shop with it. As you pick up something in one hand, such as a loaf of bread, attune your attention to the Eat Stone in your other hand. If the Eat Stone gives you YES vibes, then that bread is good for your body. If the stone gives you NO vibes, then try a different brand.

Birth Control Stone: These egg-shaped stones are kept nearby during sex. The Birth Control stone regulates the vibrations between lovers and allows for pregnancy

only if it is cosmically right. For individuals who use "natural" birth control and other high-risk methods.

Tarthu Tunga: These rare crystals from deep in the most inaccessible mountains of Tibet are used on ceremonial headdresses by high priests and priestesses and by intergalactic voyagers. The Tarthu Tunga can only be worn in the center of a massive silk and jeweled head ornament of serious proportions. Such a headdress was once worn by Tibetan oracles, and causes the wearer to stagger under its weight. When one wears a Tarthu Tunga, one becomes united with the Seventy-seven Supreme Deities of the Holy Concoction of the Elusive Spirit. This causes one to rant in the vaguest of all possible spiritual terms and to give the impression of being mighty and horrible.

Salvation Stone: Perhaps the most popular of all crystals, the Salvation Stone is simple and affordable. But it is very powerful indeed. Simply by accepting the crystal as your personal savior, you are saved, all your sins are forgiven, and you will unquestionably enter the Kingdom of Heaven. These are also known as Security Stones.

If you'd like to know more about the power of crystals, the following books may be helpful: *Getting Stoned* by Abbie Foolsgold, *Crystals for Sex and Profit* by Samantha Starbite, *The Rocky Road to Power* by Ronald Rayban, and *Pebbles for Peace* by Mahatma Wallet.

Cheap Dharma Discount Meditation Supplies

CHEAP DHARMA DISCOUNT offers a great assortment of meditation supplies by mail order from their wholesale operation at Mount Shasta, California. Whether you are an individual meditating alone in a small space or a group gathering in a huge hall, Cheap Dharma Discount has meditation supplies to match your budget and needs. The following product descriptions are taken directly from their mail order catalog.

Statues

The Golden Buddha: Made of high-quality, gold-colored styrene plastic, this Buddha has a weighted bottom and makes an excellent bookend. A slot in the top of the head also makes this holy object a fine piggy bank.

Altar Accessories

Sand-Cast Altar Candles: Shaped like small castles, these fine sand-cast candles will add grandeur to your altar. As the candles burn, the wax melts into the tower turrets. Very cool.

Silk Flowers: Sure, it's respectful to offer fresh flowers to the gods every day, but it is also expensive. These silk roses, fresias, tulips, and daffodils look like the real thing, but they don't wilt, brown, and die. Instead they look perfectly fresh and vibrant year after year.

Noisemakers

Drums: We have holy bongos, tablas, and Tibetan yak skin barrel drums. All drums are handmade from finely cut plywood and are covered with tough, Rubbermaid trash tops. These drums may be pounded incessantly during chanting or may be bashed suddenly to awaken dozing meditators.

Dharma Prods: These high-voltage rods will blast the bad karma right out of any novitiate. Sleeping students a problem? Not with the Dharma Prod. Even the doziest of meditators will sit ramrod straight, bolt upright, wide awake, after just one poke with this phaser.

Art

Prints: We offer a fine collection of Zen Buddhist Nudist Pinups, including the Dharma Dolls Calendar and the entire Nymphs of Nirvana collection.

Seating

Cushions: We carry the new La-Z-Boy Meditation Cushion with the reclining backrest and the extra soft knee pads. Models come in your choice of fabrics and colors. Additional embroidered scripture work can be ordered.

Benches: Our new Picnic Meditator and Park Meditator benches are terrific additions to backyard meditation spaces, and make excellent off-the-ground napping spaces as well. Options include drinking-glass holders and waterproof cushions.

Cheap Dharma Discount Meditation Supplies may be ordered 24 hours a day, all year long. To order or to receive a catalog, write Cheap Dharma Discount, 458 UFO Lane, Mount Shasta, CA 96067.

Floatation Tanks on Wheels

The Ultimate Driving Machine

ONE OF THE most stressful parts of anyone's day is the drive to and from work. Commuting is tough on the nervous system. It provokes feelings of rage, aggression, and helplessness. Truth be known, a bad commute can ruin an otherwise decent day.

Now there is the Floatation Tank on Wheels, a chauffeur-driven sensory deprivation tank with superb suspension, rack and pinion steering, and a 3.6-liter high-performance engine. Now, while your hired driver absorbs the stress of the road, you can float serenely in a body-temperature cocoon, either in total silence or with your favorite New Age music playing.

With the Floatation Tank on Wheels, you eliminate driver's stress as a factor in your life and turn previously annoying time into an opportunity to refresh your entire body, mind and spirit.

The Floatation Tank on Wheels is a fabulous way to start and end your business day. Take your life to a new level of balance, ease, and sublime peace with this amazing new vehicle. The Floatation Tank on Wheels is truly the Ultimate Driving Machine.

COSMO PROTECTO WATCH

BEFORE

It is estimated that the average person is bombarded by over ten thousand different vibes every day. These vibrations come in a variety of frequencies, including plenty of bad vibes that you don't need and don't want. In fact, bad vibes are the number-one cause of all illness.

Until now, all that has protected you from intrusive vibes is your own aura, which by the end of the day is usually thin and ragged.

Just when you need it most, there is the Cosmo Protecto Watch, a normal-looking wrist watch that disarms bad vibes instantly, before they affect you. This sleek, waterproof quartz crystal timepiece is your own personal peacemaker. Strap it on to your wrist and you're ready to handle vibes as thick as a coastal fog.

The patented Digitized Vibe Zapper in the Cosmo Protecto Watch offers state-of-the-art protection at a price that's affordable. And the stylish titanium exterior of your timepiece is both contemporary and durable. With the Cosmo Protecto Watch, there are no surprise vibratory intrusions. When you wear the Cosmo Protecto Watch, you'll be healthy, energetic, and confident. Available at all fine jewelers and sports outfitters.

AFTER

Horoclock

LET'S SAY THAT you've had your astrological chart done. Most responsible adults these days have done exactly that. But when you got home, did you remember all the little details that your reader explained? Is your midheaven trine your ascendant in Pisces, or is your eighth house in a bundle configuration? Horoclock is the daily astrological reminder that lets you know exactly what's going on in the stars and tells you what to do about it. Horoclock is a computerized sleep alarm clock that provides a daily verbal astrological update. You type in your name and the date, time, and location of your birth, and the clock does the rest. Then you set Horoclock like a regular sleep alarm, and let it go to work for you.

When you are awakened by the Cosmic Tone alarm, a computer voice will tell you everything you need to know about your horoscope for the day. "Neptune is crossing Uranus. Mars is square your Scorpio. Your subconscious mind is about to erupt. Stay in bed. Do not go out today or accept any phone calls. Today rates as a 2 for you. Repeat, do not go out." If you are about to travel, Horoclock can give you a forecast for however long you will be away. "Tomorrow is an excellent day to travel. Your Mercury is in Leo, which is very good for business. Your Venus is in Sagittarius on Wednesday. It is a superior time to meet people. Prepare to be stimulated!"

With Horoclock, you can make wise personal and business decisions, based on the position of the stars. You need never be ignorant of the cosmos again. If you want to take full advantage of the benefits of astrology, Horoclock is the product for you. Each timepiece comes with Cosmic Tone Alarm or is programmable for New Age music. Horoclock brings the heavens to you each morning.

Socially Enlightened Credit Cards

IF YOU DON'T carry a socially enlightened credit card, you are living in the past. These credit cards offer you, the bearer, the unique opportunity to donate to the charity of your choice with each transaction you make. For example, if you wish to give to public radio, your local station probably has an arrangement with VISA or MasterCard by which you can carry a card bearing that station's call letters. Every time you use the card, a small amount of money will automatically go to public radio.

Socially enlightened credit cards are springing up like blades of grass in the morning dew. It is now possible to give to the group or fund of your choice, however small or out of the way that organization may be. This means that every day you can give to your charity of choice. Or you can carry several cards with you and give to a variety of causes as the mood strikes you.

But not all cards divert funds to soft, left-of-center groups like Greenpeace, Oxfam, and Sierra Club. Republicans can be socially responsible too. Here is a partial list of socially responsible credit cards that may be new to you.

MoralCard: The Moral Majority may be neither, but they sure need money. Funds go directly to Bible publishing, Christian Evangelical Television, and gasoline for the rides at Heritage Theme Park.

NRA Card: Shoot straight from the hip every time you use this card. Support our national right to arm bears, to shoot household intruders dead, to carry a pistol in public, and to blast road signs to hell and back on a Saturday night.

ChinaCard: As you know, every year the President and the First Lady entertain thousands of important guests at the White House. Even with the best of care, a few pieces of china dinnerware are likely to chip or break. With the ChinaCard you can contribute to much needed china for the White House table in this time of government spending cuts.

ContraCard: What a sticky pickle Ollie North and his cronies got into over the Contra arms deal! With ContraCard you have a means to fund anti-Sandinista forces and to keep our fine leaders out of jail. With ContraCard your donations go directly to the same medical supplies that were provided with Irangate funds. Supplies like hand-held rocket launchers, infrared sniping gear, plastic explosives, and razor wire are needed to keep the Contras healthy.

Socially Enlightened Credit Cards are an ingenious way to donate continuously and regularly to noble causes that badly need your help.

The Harmonica Virgins

IN A WORLD of copies and replicas, this is a one-of-a-kind original. The 1988 Harmonica Virgins Calendar is out, and it's outstanding!

What's the fuss about a calendar? This is *the* Mayan calendar, the only accurate chart of the earth's evolution. The Mayans figured out long ago that our humble planet is passing through a giant cosmic beam and that within about thirty years we'll be out of the beam, in perfect attunement and harmony with the rest of the galaxy. Great news!

The Harmonica Virgins Calendar chronicles our voyage through the beam, month by month. The calendar, which is profusely annotated, will teach you about the Hunab Ku, the magical filaments that extend from your belly button. You'll learn the thirteen epochs of the cosmic beam, and you'll pick up obscure Mayan lore.

Most important, though, you'll be able to feast your eyes upon the lovely Harmonica Virgins, twelve high-minded, firm-breasted nymphs, ready to excite and delight you. These are the original Harmonica Virgins, sumptuous little ladies with silken skin, bedroom eyes, and devastating bodies! You've never seen a calendar that even comes close to this all-star lineup of pre-Colombian cuties. See Miss July perched upon a pyramid. Eye Miss October as she mounts a Chac Mool. Every month is a work of art, ready for a permanent spot on the wall of your home or shop.

The Harmonica Virgins Calendar is a don't-miss. To order yours, call toll-free 1-777-UNDRESS.

ORDER NOW!!!

REINCARNATION
Life Insurance Policy

To take the fear out of death, Diamond Sutra Life and Casualty is making this once-in-a-blue-moon offer for Reincarnation Life Insurance—a comprehensive insurance program that keeps you covered after you've dropped your body.

Premiums are calculated by comparing the incarnation you apply for with the incarnation you have actually earned. (Just pay the one-time charge below and we will bill the premium to you in your next life, when you can afford it.) If the discrepancy is great, your premiums will be higher than if you make a realistic request. But, in either case, Diamond Sutra will see that you are rescued from your just desserts and given the lifetime accommodations provided by your Reincarnation Life Insurance Policy.

To receive your policy, simply fill out the application form provided in IN SEARCH OF THE NEW AGE (see page 23, or make a copy), and send it, along with a processing fee of $12.50, to:

> **Reincarnation Life Insurance**
> **c/o Destiny Books**
> **One Park Street**
> **Rochester, VT 05767**

We will send you a personalized Reincarnation Life Insurance Policy. (Also makes a great gift—just tell us who to send it to.) Allow 4 weeks for delivery.